DRIVEN

Business Strategy, Human Actions, and the Creation of Wealth

DRIVEN

Business Strategy, Human Actions, and the Creation of Wealth

Mark L. Frigo   Joel Litman

Edition 1.0

Strategy & Execution, L.L.C.

Library of Congress Control Number: 2008900012
ISBN: 978-0-9814573-0-7
S&E No.   D:bs-ha-atcow-071229

Printed in the United States of America.

Contents

Part Five: The Foundations

Part Six: Conclusion

Acknowledgements

More people have contributed to this book's creation than we could list. For years, we have been supported, assisted, and encouraged by many people and organizations.

We give thanks to our clients and colleagues including those at Credit Suisse, HOLT, and the people in and around the HOLT client network who have generously provided insights and analysis, as well as use of the invaluable CFROI® framework and database.

We give special thanks to those who have supported The Center for Strategy, Execution, and Valuation and so many in and around the Kellstadt Graduate School of Business at DePaul University.

We sincerely thank the business leaders, investors, analysts, directors, and students who have participated in the seminars and courses conducted around the world over the last several years. Those who have actively used the framework in their organizations have contributed valuable feedback, criticisms, and kudos.

Most of all, we appreciate the support of our friends and families. We thank you for your tireless support, encouragement, endless conversations, and everything that has led to this book. We also thank you for your support in the future efforts of this book and framework, particularly for the benefit it can have for others.

Preface

This book is about Return Driven Strategy™, a framework for planning and evaluating businesses that can help people to generate wealth for themselves and for society. If ever a congruency was realized between "making the world a better place" and "getting wealthy," we believe those principles are described herein.

The framework describes the plans and actions that drive returns for all the constituents of a firm. These actions lead to the creation of wealth for customers, employees, shareholders, and society. In planning, building, and running businesses, Return Driven Strategy has helped leaders to choose what actions to take and when to take them.

We started this journey over a decade ago. We asked ourselves what we could learn by studying the experiences of companies good and bad, exceptional and exceptionally flawed, as well as those stuck in average levels of performance.

Our intention was to describe how companies achieved periods of sustained, high performance so that the activities can be better understood and adapted by others. We also wondered if the simple absence of these factors would explain the activities that lead to certain doom or leave firms commoditized in mediocrity.

Driven is written for organizations and individuals who want to create more wealth by improving how they plan their businesses and take action. We believe passionately in these ideas, as do many people whom we have had the honor of working with over the years. The ideas, tenets, and strategies in this book have been tested and refined with executives, managers, investors, board members, entrepreneurs, and many other colleagues.

Whether a firm is large or small, composed of one person or millions, results can be described by the cash flows the firm uses and generates. Cash flows most objectively describe the amount of society's valuable resources that a company absorbs. They also help to describe a firm's success in using those resources to fulfill certain needs of society.

We were fortunate to be able to use one of the most powerful, and un-doubtedly most comprehensive cash flow performance databases available, that provided by Credit Suisse HOLT. With this, we were able to screen through and study tens of thousands of firms in over 50 nations, with as much as several decades of cash flow history and forecasts.

High-performance businesses are run by managers who think and act differently. These companies have found ways to escape from the grind of commoditization and competition by focusing on the right goals. Those goals are specifically described, communicated, and aligned with society's needs; then translated into the right strategies around customers and offerings. "Return-driven" firms conscientiously develop unique capabilities and resources that allow them to deliver offerings in ways no other firm can.

We believe that every business, large or small, can benefit from this book and can find a way to apply the concepts and strategies in *Driven* for their own benefit, and for the communities around them.

We invite you to read this book and to use the concepts and strategies to guide you toward higher levels of performance, creating wealth for you and for others along the way.

An Overview of Return Driven Strategy

Return Driven Strategy™ provides an understanding of what specific types of business activities drive the highest levels of wealth-creation. With its foundations in one of the most advanced financial modeling frameworks, it provides a powerful tool for forecasting the potential for a particular business initiative to create wealth or destroy it.

Very different ideas about what makes a business successful

The following is a sample of the concepts explained in *Driven*. These often reveal misunderstandings about business strategy that have led many companies to destroy value, or have severely limited the wealth that could have been created.

- *Businesses with great products are often not great businesses (Explained in Chapter Two)*

- *When to shrink and grow rich – or grow and be poor (Chapter Three)*

- *Why "first mover advantage" is often anything but (Chapter Twelve)*

- *The undeniable financial impact of business ethics on performance (Chapter One)*

- *"Being different" is a by-product of great strategy, not a focus (Chapter Two)*

- *How a monopoly, generally so desired, will cause valuations to stagnate (Chapter Three)*

- *The difference between a great company and a great stock (Chapter Fourteen)*

- *The real customer needs are seldom the obvious ones (Chapter Two)*

- *How treating employees as customers generates higher returns to all constituents (Chapter Nine)*

- *Which is more important, strategy or execution? Both. (Chapter Four)*

Some of these concepts can come as a surprise, but the underlying financial and practical support for them is substantial.

An outline of the framework

Of everything that Return Driven Strategy offers to its users, a primary benefit is better resource allocation: the prioritization of time and efforts in planning, analysis, and implementation.

As projects compete for capital, time, and resources, Return Driven Strategy can assist management in choosing and timing the actions that are best poised for achieving the organization's goals.

The framework appears in pyramid form, in order of importance in long-term performance and valuation impact.

The following is a summary of the framework *and the book*. The first eleven chapters in *Driven* focus on the Eleven Tenets and the final three chapters cover the Three Foundations.

Tenet One

Ethically Maximize Wealth

In order to achieve wealth, management must first define it explicitly. The firm should then align all of its activities toward that goal of wealth-creation as defined. Top-performing managers are very clear about what they are trying to achieve and how they intend to get there.

In order to create wealth, one must first not destroy it. A mountain of financial evidence shows that gross unethical conduct is a business risk that does not bear a justifying reward. The definition and pursuit of wealth must fall within the ethical parameters of the communities in which the business operates. Failure to operate ethically risks everything that the managers have and hope to achieve. An incredibly extensive history of business valuations proves this concept clearly.

Tenets Two and Three

Fulfill Otherwise Unmet Customer Needs
Target Appropriate Customer Groups

The path to high-performance and wealth-creation is through the customer – by fulfilling the unmet needs of lots of customers, in ways no one else can.

Customer satisfaction or quality ratings do not necessarily translate into superior financial performance. Unfortunately, the world is littered with businesses with mediocre performance despite those businesses providing the *best* products. Real pricing power stems from providing offerings that are greatly needed and yet have no substitute. Pricing power leads to higher returns.

The term 'quality' means very different things to different people. A person chooses one product or service over another because of a set of attributes that reside in the mind of the customer, which may be totally different from what would appear obvious at first. High-performance firms reap the benefits of understanding the psychological reasons behind customer purchases.

Return-driven businesses target customer groups that support the wealth-creation goals as they have been defined. If investors define wealth as a stable net income stream, then the firm needs to target stable customer groups with consistent needs. High investment growth opportunities may require targeting high growth customer groups, but where returns can be far more volatile and uncertain. Stability in income and maximum increases in income are generally not achievable at the same time.

Achievement of high returns hinges on being the dominant provider of offerings to the appropriate customer group.

Tenets Four, Five, and Six

Deliver Offerings
Innovate Offerings
Brand Offerings

Three core competencies form the driving force behind the creation of the right offerings for the right customers. No single competency is sufficient. These must be balanced as the customer groups and customer needs would require. A business should not 'choose' a particular competency, but continually adjust its competencies as the higher tenets would direct.

Deliver Offerings: High-performance firms deliver offerings to customers as planned, promised, and expected. This does not mean perfect execution every time. It means understanding the expectations that customers have for fulfilling a particular need, and meeting those delivery requirements.

In some industries such as retail, customers may be satisfied with goods being mispriced one in a hundred times, so long as the lowest possible price is received overall. In other industries, such as vehicle braking systems, one fault in a million is one too many.

Innovate Offerings: Customers' unmet needs change over time as do the methods available for fulfilling them. When customer needs change rapidly, business offerings can quickly become obsolete. Rapid innovation is necessary to change with them. Innovation of offerings is the solution to protecting existing markets and expanding into new ones.

Brand Offerings: Branding is an important competency when brands act as bridges. Successful firms create a bridge between the customers' knowledge of the offering and their explicit awareness of their unmet need. Done in an emotionally compelling way, purchases can be induced at pricing levels that reflect the business's efforts.

Together, these three competencies are necessary for driving high returns at any firm and in any industry. The right balance of the three is dependent on the higher tenets.

Tenets Seven through Eleven

Partner Deliberately
Map and Redesign Processes
Engage Employees and Others
Balance Focus and Options
Communicate Holistically

High-performance firms display five specific types of activities for enhancing their ability to achieve the higher tenets. While the same activities appear in lower-performing firms, the difference lies in the degree of alignment of these activities with the higher tenets.

For example, lower-performing firms engage in partnering and other activities indiscriminately, taking up valuable resources that result in limited benefit to any of the firm's constituents. However, when each of these tenets is used for the specific purpose of better accomplishing the competency tenets, higher performance results.

Three Foundations of Business Strategy

The three foundations form the base of the pyramid. They apply to each tenet. Achievement of each tenet requires consideration of the three foundations.

Genuine Assets

The Eleven Tenets are the *verbs* of a successful business. Genuine Assets are the *nouns* that create competitive advantages and sustainability of high performance. Genuine Assets are unique tangible or intangible assets that are difficult or impossible to copy. Examples include unique patent portfolios, exclusive customer relationships, proprietary customer information, and key geographic locations.

When businesses create and deploy Genuine Assets in their activities, they greatly increase the potential to create unassailable advantages. A business should engage in a particular activity using a Genuine Asset, such that without that Genuine Asset, the activity cannot be copied.

For example, a Genuine Asset, such as a monopoly on vending machines, could create situations where other businesses cannot target the customers at those locations. Or, a Genuine Asset may be an exclusive partnership and right to distribute a particular product, such that no other distributor can sell that product. A set of patents is an example of a Genuine Asset that makes it difficult or impossible to recreate a particular offering for some fixed amount of time. Genuine Assets are the building blocks of sustainable competitive advantage throughout the entire pyramid of tenets.

Vigilance to Forces of Change

Dynamic threats and opportunities arise for businesses regularly. The adage is that *change is a constant*. To succeed, business activities need to be continually reevaluated. Three distinct areas where forces of change arise require close watching. These three areas are the following:

- Governmental and regulatory change
- Demographic and cultural shifts
- Scientific and technological breakthroughs

Formerly great businesses have been decimated by forces of change that can be described within the context of these three categories. Meanwhile, many businesses have launched and made trillions of dollars by capitalizing on the same forces. Vigilance of change is necessary, adjusting the pursuit of each tenet accordingly.

Disciplined Performance Measurement and Valuation

This foundation is the underlying bedrock of all great business planning, analysis, and performance. Business flaws can frequently be tied to misunderstandings of how business plans, implementation, results, and valuation are quantitatively linked. An inability to understand what drives valuations, particularly in the stock market, will cause managers to do the wrong things.

Performance Measurement: The complexity of financial statements of even simple businesses can make it difficult for users of those financials to understand the economic reality of a company's performance. Even simply knowing whether or not a business's performance is *directionally* good or bad can be difficult to discern from the financials.

A few statements can summarize the recognition of the importance of performance measurement at firms. These include, *"If you can't measure it, you can't manage it," "What gets measured gets done," "People do what they are paid to do,"* and *"It's better to be approximately right than precisely wrong."* Measuring the right things at the right times is an important aspect of building a business planning framework such as Return Driven Strategy.

Strategic Valuation: While performance measures gauge what has happened historically or what is happening now, valuation is about forecasting the performance of the future. This brings about an entirely new set of issues. Concepts arise like business life cycles and the opportunity cost of capital employed. These are necessary to understanding the value of a firm.

Foremost of the misconceptions in business analysis and valuation is the too-common belief that companies that see dramatic increases in stock price are necessarily great companies. This simply isn't the case. Great companies often have average stock performance. Relatively poorer performers will often have great stock price appreciation, even over several years.

With this knowledge, one can recognize *"The difference between a great company and a great stock,"* and the problems that arise when managers confuse one for the other.

Different Analysis, Different Conclusions

The financial discipline underlying this business strategy research is not inconsequential. Many firms that receive substantial press for being highly admired companies are found to have admirable public relations skills, but less than respectable financial performance.

At times, companies regarded as "great" have in actuality been *great turnarounds*. Firms like this are worthy of study for how to dig a business out of a hole, but are greatly lacking as cases for high value achievement.

Many businesses don't receive a lot of press, yet quietly generate cash flow returns that amaze investors. They produce offerings built by engaged employees and partners that are subsequently purchased by customers who voluntarily pay high prices to fulfill their needs in ways they could not otherwise. Examples of these types of firms are used to explain the concepts behind Return Driven Strategy.

People can make better decisions when they understand the connection between business planning, business actions, and wealth-creation. As authors and practitioners, we hope to provide an easy-to-understand, straightforward approach to business planning and evaluation. We respectfully offer *Driven* not only as an explanation, but also as a field guide for reference.

DRIVEN

Part One

The Commitment Tenet

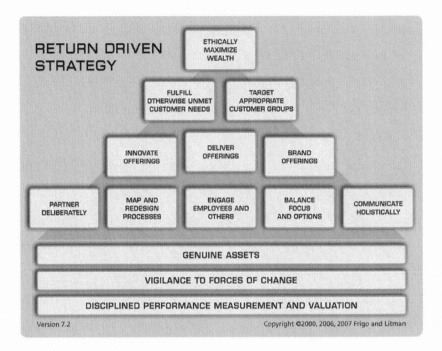

1

Tenet One

Ethically Maximize Wealth

This overriding, first tenet of business strategy is the "top of the house" issue for businesses that seek to create wealth. Of all the various planning and actions in which a firm could engage, none have such a high impact on performance and valuation as this tenet. Successful firms do the following:

- Define wealth explicitly in terms of monetary and non-monetary goals, timetables, and acceptable risk levels

- Commit managers to wealth-creation as defined, and align the entire organization's plans and activities toward the wealth-creation goals

- Act with the knowledge that in the long-term, investors' wealth is dependent on improving the livelihood of the other constituents of the firm, particularly the employees and customers

- Operate within the ethical boundaries of the communities served – as those communities would define, or all wealth potential is put at unnecessary risk

- Employ Genuine Assets to generate and sustain ethical wealth-creation for the long-term

- Be watchful for forces of change that may require a redefinition of wealth and/or a realignment of its pursuit in order to remain committed to achievement of this tenet

- Specifically identify how wealth will be measured, and define all monetary definitions in terms of cash flow performance and potential long-term cash flow generation

The Johnson & Johnson Credo

Johnson & Johnson has created tremendous levels of wealth for its constituents. During the period studied, cash flow returns and growth rates were consistently more than double or triple corporate averages. Returns to shareholders exceeded very healthy market averages over more than two decades.

The firm's credo belies its strategy, one totally consistent with the Return Driven Strategy framework, and specifically, Tenet One. The credo aligns the firm toward specific goals that help the firm Ethically Maximize Wealth. In the credo, note the attention to all the constituents of the firm, the ethical considerations, and the implied long-term timetables. (See Exhibit 1.1 on the following page).

Return to investors in terms of cash flow is only one measure of how Johnson & Johnson has achieved 'sound profit.' The firm exhibits high levels of customer need fulfillment, as the high returns on investment can only be achieved by offering customers something that they cannot get elsewhere. These generate higher shareholder returns. In other words, the company's products are unique to a degree that customers freely pay prices for JNJ goods and services that allow the firm to generate such high cash flows.

Because of the long history and success of this credo, it becomes a genuine asset to the firm in sustaining its ability to achieve Tenet One. It highlights the importance of all of the business's communities in the creation of wealth. It also defines the firm's measures of wealth, and the activities that would pursue it. In fact, the credo addresses most of the tenets of Return Driven Strategy in a single mission statement.

Exhibit 1.1

<u>*JNJ CREDO*</u>

We believe our first responsibility is to the doctors, nurses and patients, to mothers and fathers and all others who use our products and services.

In meeting their needs everything we do must be of high quality. We must constantly strive to reduce our costs in order to maintain reasonable prices.

Customers' orders must be serviced promptly and accurately. Our suppliers and distributors must have an opportunity to make a fair profit.

We are responsible to our employees, the men and women who work with us throughout the world. Everyone must be considered as an individual. We must respect their dignity and recognize their merit. They must have a sense of security in their jobs.

Compensation must be fair and adequate, and working conditions clean, orderly and safe. We must be mindful of ways to help our employees fulfill their family responsibilities.

Employees must feel free to make suggestions and complaints. There must be equal opportunity for employment, development and advancement for those qualified. We must provide competent management, and their actions must be just and ethical.

We are responsible to the communities in which we live and work and to the world community as well. We must be good citizens – support good works and charities and bear our fair share of taxes. We must encourage civic improvements and better health and education. We must maintain in good order the property we are privileged to use, protecting the environment and natural resources. Our final responsibility is to our stockholders.

Business must make a sound profit. We must experiment with new ideas. Research must be carried on, innovative programs developed and mistakes paid for.

New equipment must be purchased, new facilities provided and new products launched. Reserves must be created to provide for adverse times. When we operate according to these principles, the stockholders should realize a fair return.

Wealth is maximized through the people

In the credo, one notices references to the major constituents of the firm. This is for good reason and necessary for a firm that strives to be a high-performer. People vote for their favorite businesses every day. They freely choose – and thereby vote economically.

- **Businesses** are free to choose what offerings to provide
- **Customers** are free to choose where they spend their money
- **Employees** are free to choose where they work and for whom
- **Investors** are free to choose where to invest their capital

In the long-term, the most successful businesses win by being a key central exchange point for each of the above constituents. As each group voluntarily acts to fulfill its needs, the firm acting as a central point of that exchange can create incredible levels of wealth. In an economically free society – *in an economic democracy* – the constituents drive the cash flows.

Customers express their pleasure or displeasure economically. They vote with their spending. They drive the firm's revenues higher when the firm provides what the customers need. They pay higher relative prices when the business can provide offerings they need that they can't get elsewhere. If a firm can deliver something that uniquely fulfills their most pressing needs, high levels of cash flow to the business.

Employees vote with their time. They reward the business with their efforts, choosing to work at firms that provide what they need, always something far more than just annual compensation. Employees flock to organizations where they are paid in ways that they as employees determine most valued. In exchange, the business receives their effort.

Investors vote with their investments. Business managers are tasked with processing inputs of time, effort, and other resources and producing offerings that customers flock to. As the judges of this process, investors reward businesses when they see the potential for higher levels of succeeding with customers. With publicly traded companies, an increasing demand for shares of the business drives higher stock prices.

Managers that drive businesses to achieve highest levels of cash flow performance and valuations are those that fulfill the needs of all their constituents, not just one.

Is wealth-creation ethical?

When the needs of the various constituents of a business are being met in voluntary exchange, the communities generally see the firm's activities functioning within ethical parameters. Woe to the society that deems wealth-creation a bad thing, or believes that wealth is only taken and never created.

In centrally managed economies, the government takes away basic economic freedoms. In these countries, the leaders have decided that the government is best to decide exactly what products companies should produce, what products customers should purchase, and where employees should work. When compared against centrally managed economies, free societies have displayed better human conditions on almost every measure imaginable, from education to healthcare to basic human rights. Ironically, centrally-managed governments are often originally established with the support of the populace.

For those who have not yet researched the implications of such an issue, the late Milton Friedman offers an undeniable set of evidence in his works. A thorough study over the last several thousand years of the gross differences in human conditions between centrally-planned economies and economically free societies leaves no doubt as to which is best for its citizens.

Do societies view wealth-creation as an ethical endeavor? The societies that support economic freedoms in the pursuit of wealth-creation and need fulfillment have prospered. The ones that don't have suffered dramatically.

Wealth-creation that benefits the constituents

Bart Madden is author of several publications including the book, *CFROI® Valuation*. Many of the HOLT community of investors, managers, and practitioners affectionately regard him as the 'father of the CFROI calculation.' Few have studied the economic impact of corporate actions as much as Madden. In his monograph, *Maximizing Shareholder Value and the Greater Good,* Bart commented on the value of wealth-creation in this way,

> *"...specific company track records reveal that the long-term, mutual interests of customers, employees, and shareholders are served by the "maximize shareholder value" guide for taking corporate actions. Clear, concrete examples such as Bethlehem Steel (showing economic wealth and job destruction) or Medtronic (showing economic wealth and job creation) may convince some people of this solid ground when abstract arguments about the greater good have failed."*

Votes can be for or against

The power of the firm's constituents can drive a company's performance and valuation to new highs or to record lows in very short order. Certain types of business activities can draw great levels of anger from these groups. While businesses appear to be resilient to mistakes of many kinds, nothing appears to negatively impact a firm as much as when these groups decide that a business has engaged in *gross unethical conduct.*

Some may find it strange or even "weak" to begin a book about strategy and valuation with a discussion of business ethics. Some have even questioned how analysis based on cash flows can result in such a finding.

The need to address business ethics at the beginning of business strategy is driven by thorough cash flow analysis, across thousands of companies over 30+ years.

It's not that companies that operate within the ethics of their communities are guaranteed success. They aren't. Instead, the valuation analysis shows bluntly that the companies that engage in *gross unethical conduct* are the companies that experience *the deepest valuation losses.*

Business success requires *staying in business*

Warren Buffett is often quoted with the following:
- "Rule No. 1: Never lose money."
- "Rule No. 2: Never forget rule No. 1"

Firms that exhibit gross unethical conduct are ones that lose money because its constituents will refuse to do business with the firm or even sue the firm. No matter how great the firm's assets, technologies, historical performance, or resources, the firm can still lose phenomenal amounts of money by doing things in violation of the communities' values – whatever those may be.

Avoiding the downside

If owners and management wish to be concerned with good or great firm performance, they must first occupy themselves with not destroying value in the first place. Management should put at least as much effort in ensuring against the downside as in working for the upside.

Companies strive for and pride themselves on even 3% to 5% annual increases in revenues, margins, or relative stock price increases. Placing so much focus on incremental gains can only make sense if the firm also puts controls in place to avoid excessively high risks. The risks to valuations of gross unethical conduct are obvious: huge drops in performance in a few weeks, even days.

No business can be separated or insulated from the society in which it is immersed. In today's global economy, a belief that a business can profit for a long duration at the expense of any major constituency goes against the odds of healthy wealth generation. Extensive cash flow analysis exhibits that over and over again.

In the short-term, incremental successes can be possible by cutting corners and robbing Peter to pay Paul. But over time, the pressures on the other parts of society will come back to haunt the organization.

If, as Warren Buffett says, not losing money is the first rule of investment success, so then is ethical conduct the first rule of business strategy.

Exhibit 1.2, on the following page, shows examples of companies where one or more constituents determined that there had been gross unethical conduct. There is a consistent theme across all of these examples and hundreds more like them. Each of these firms violated the ethical parameters of the communities in which they operated in a significant way. Consequently their valuations were severely damaged if not destroyed.

Tyco's CEO was convicted of misappropriating hundreds of millions of dollars for personal use. Worldcom publicly reported activities that did not reflect the real expenses or assets of the firm with misstatements in the billions of dollars. Enron used special entities to record revenues that did not exist and funneled company funds into the hands of unscrupulous individuals.

Worldcom and Enron went bankrupt. The valuation of TYC fell to a level from which the firm may never recover. The conduct of these firms destroyed wealth in the billions; people lost their jobs, their savings, and even their retirements. Not only did management lose, but society also lost.

Punishment is economic and overwhelming

Of the companies listed in the table, many had truly innovative business models. Many leveraged new technologies in unique ways. Most had been growing their businesses with new offerings. However, the negative impact on a firm's value from unethical conduct overwhelms the otherwise healthy attributes of the business. Constituents punish with severe economic implications.

Exhibit 1.2

These companies display what happens when firms are deemed by their constituents to have engaged in gross unethical conduct. In some cases, investors sue the firm's management team; in others, customers boycott the firm's offerings.

Over long-term horizons, the firms have trouble hiring the best candidates who would not want to be associated with the firm. Gross unethical conduct has the potential to bring attacks from these groups that the firm cannot defend. The result can be bankruptcy, falling stock prices, and performance that may never completely recover.

Company	Unethical Practice Deemed by Constituents
Enron	Defrauded employees & investors
Ford	Refused to incur expense to fix defective Pinto
Lucent	Fraudulent accounting
Mercury Interactive	Stock options scandal
Parmalat	Defrauded investors
Phar Mor	Executive management embezzlement
Tyco	Fraudulent acquisition accounting
Waste Management	Fraudulent accounting
WorldCom	Fraudulent accounting
ZZZZ Best	Fraud through forgery & theft

Other examples in the past have included Adelphia, Global Crossing, Cendant, Xerox, Computer Associates, Rite Aid, and many more.

When **customers** feel that they have been victimized by a firm, they respond in class action lawsuits, boycotting its offerings with public displays, and simply avoiding their goods and services.

Few businesses can succeed in the long-term with disgruntled **employees.** Workers will restrict their time and creativity at companies where they feel ethically slighted. They then work dispassionately until vacating the firm for a better situation, as they perceive it. Employees revolt through work slowdowns and poor service to customers. When the offenses are serious, employees unionize and strike and picket, file class action lawsuits, express dissatisfaction directly to customers, and many other things that can stall an organization.

The **public** exerts an influence on firm activities. The general public, through the government, will punish firms by regulating against themselves and sometimes forcing themselves out of business.

Investors withhold their monetary capital from firms with questionable business practices, those that create risk which exceeds the opportunity. They closely watch the activities of the firm, recognizing how gross unethical conduct will have a myriad of bad side-effects as described above.

One thing for certain, investors do not like being lied to or cheated. They retaliate faster than any other group by pulling investments from the firm as stock prices trade downward. In the first sizable wave of financial restatements following the Enron scandals, firms which restated their financials – essentially, getting caught misreporting their financial activity – saw their stock price drop 10% to 20% in just a few days' time. When management owns stock in the firm, that kind of drop hits them where they feel it. In more severe cases, investors also engage in lawsuits.

Again, it's not that being ethical guarantees a firm's success. The point is that cheating, lying to, or stealing from any of the major constituencies raises the risk of absolute financial failure. Being ethical is necessary just to be in the game.

The firms' constituents define ethics, not the firms

Everyone else is doing it. To compete, we need to do it too.

In the past, this defense has been made to justify actions later found to be grossly unethical. People involved in these actions will often admit that at the time, they had a feeling that something was wrong, but did not do anything about it.

One test for ethical behavior is known as the 'mob test.' Essentially, if a manager is using the 'everyone is doing it' phrase to justify an action, it usually means that something's potentially wrong with it from an ethical standpoint. This leads to a second question as to whether or not it's grossly unethical from the standpoint of the firm's constituents. If so, the long-term health of the business could be in jeopardy.

In the phrase, *'everyone is doing it,'* the term, 'everyone,' usually refers to the manager's peers or competitors. If four out of five firms are willing to record revenues that don't actually exist, in the short term their stock prices might beat out the one company who reports revenues honestly. In the long term, the fact that a majority of the firms were all committing the same fraud hasn't been a viable defense in the eyes of the public.

Investors, employees, customers, and vendors will find ways to retaliate against behavior deemed unethical as they define, and *not as the industry's management teams would choose to define it.* Industry leaders saying that a particular activity is "ok" doesn't make it so, no matter how many firms agree.

Changing communities, changing ethics

Ethical parameters change based on geography, cultures, ethnicity, size and type of business, and change over time. Any business that wishes to succeed must find ways to understand the boundaries and limitations of the groups it seeks to do business with. What's ethical in one part of the world may be considered unethical in another. What is ethical to investors may not be considered ethical to consumers. All of these communities' parameters must be taken into consideration.

The "public display test" is a valuable tool for considering these issues. In this test, management is asked to imagine that a particular business activity is being reported on the front page of a newspaper. Would management suspect a backlash from readers of the paper? In most cases where firms have been punished for a particular activity, this test would have caused managers to rethink the activity beforehand.

When performing this test, one can imagine the headline on a specific newspaper's front page. If the firm has constituents in France, than the newspaper headline might be considered in *Le Monde*. If the business intends to sell to customers in Asia, then picturing the topic as the main story in the *Asia Wall Street Journal* may be better, and then consider the reaction of the local constituents to that headline. It is folly to assume that all customer groups have similar concepts of what is ethical business behavior. A great manager would think through the long-term impact on (and from) each constituency when faced with ethical dilemmas.

After ethical standards are understood, wealth needs to be defined

In order to create wealth, one needs to define it. Success to one may be failure to another. Businesses easily fail when the organization lacks an understanding of what the real goals of the business are intended to be. The word, 'wealth' has different meanings to different owners. The first task for every management team is to understand and define what 'wealth-creation' means, and align everyone and everything the business does, with that meaning.

"This is my company. I built it. I'll run it how I please."

In many privately held businesses, the owners *are* the managers. One Midwest bakery asked a group of consultants how to improve their business. After product and market studies, the consultants found that the owner/managers could potentially sell their business to a large global food company.

22

It was an interesting concept, full of natural benefits to both sides of the acquisition. The global firm could have taken the small bakery's brand and distribution to national levels in ways the regional firm's management did not have the ability to do on its own.

The owner/managers would have received cash so substantial that the annual interest on the acquisition price would have dwarfed the firm's then current annual profits. It sounded like an incredible opportunity for wealth-creation, benefiting all.

The consultants were asked to meet the owner/managers on their factory floor. There, the consultants' recommendations were summarily rejected. The owner/managers were standing in the bakery, in full chef outfits with aprons, and puffy chef hats, covered in flour and sugar. Their response was simple and telling, "That sounds like a lot of money. But if we sell our business… then what would we do?"

It's very difficult to second guess owners for doing exactly what they want with their business, pursuing what they believe is valuable to them. So long as they are the owners, the definition of wealth is their right.

The consultants failed to define what wealth meant to the owner/managers in the first place. For some it's money. For others, it is something else.

Fiduciary duties of managers who are not the owners

The issue changes dramatically when the managers of the firm are not 100% owners. At times, the business manager continues to pursue a goal that is inconsistent with the goals of the investors.
Investors play an important role in making sure society's resources are not unnecessarily squandered. When managers choose goals that are inconsistent with the owners or investors, they circumvent that role.

To succeed, a manager has to know what success looks like, so-to-speak, and wealth goals need to be defined. The investors who provide the firm with its resources are the ones with the role – and the right – to define those wealth goals.

Even the goals of publicly-traded companies can differ

Even at companies with publicly-traded stocks, the definition of wealth can change as the profiles of the company's investors change. Retirees who are dependent on a company's annual dividends may want year-to-year consistency in those dividend payouts. They will seek to invest in firms with very stable businesses.

Meanwhile, other investors may seek highest gains in stock appreciation. These investors would rather not receive dividends, but prefer the company to reinvest all of its earnings into high-growth, high potential initiatives. They are willing to accept high levels of volatility and risk for a larger potential payoff in the future.

Managers need to very carefully define what "shareholder wealth" means to the shareholders (or the owners) of the firm. Even when firms have specifically delineated their wealth goals, they are still difficult to achieve. When goals are not defined, 'success' becomes impossible, naturally.

Defining monetary wealth in cash flow terms

Financial goals are best defined by cash flow targets and cash flow analysis. By comparing cash flow returns against the opportunity costs of the investments made, one can determine whether or not resources were used efficiently. In other words, managers can then look at their performance relative to others who might have used the same level of society's resources, as defined by the dollar amount of investments made in the firm.

What are the cash flow returns of the business?

At a high level, there is a perfect analogy between examining company performance and understanding the performance of a bank savings account. Asking "What are the cash flow returns of the company?" is just like asking "What is the interest rate on the bank account?"

What is the cost of the assets required to run the business?

Every business requires some amount of investment to fund equipment, inventory, receivables, and other assets. These investments have a real opportunity cost. The cash spent on investments in the business could have been invested elsewhere. Therefore, the average return that could have been received elsewhere is regarded as the opportunity cost.

This 'opportunity cost' of investments can be viewed just like the average available savings account interest rate. Just as a person compares the interest they are receiving in their personal savings account against the interest rates available elsewhere, so too should managers compare the return on investment they generate against the rates of returns that other businesses are generating.

Does the business invest and reinvest in accordance with the rate of return they expect to be generating?

Every person knows that if a particular savings account is getting a higher interest rate than others, they should reinvest their interest in the account, and move money from other savings accounts into that one. Similarly, every business manager should seek to reinvest when rates of return can be generated higher than the opportunity cost, and disinvest (shrink) the business when returns are below.

All financial goals of a business need to be based on these basic wealth-creation rules. Any financial definitions of wealth which are inconsistent with the above concepts are dubious and can steer the organization into poor performance. The Appendix includes a more thorough discussion.

Sailing all ships as one fleet

It's difficult enough to create wealth, more so when various parts of a business aren't working together. High-performance firms align the entire organization toward the goals of wealth-creation as they had previously defined.

"Upper management says we're an entrepreneurial organization. But many of us think we're just a bunch of business units going ten different directions because upper management hasn't laid out a plan for exactly what they want."

Simply telling people to *'grow revenues and profits'* is insufficient in aligning an organization. Mission statements, such as Johnson & Johnson's Credo, help to detail specific objectives that align with the overall goals.

The fleet takes the direction from the head of the fleet, from the tone of management. After understanding and defining 'wealth-creation,' management must point everything the business does toward it.

Form DEF14A:
The most important report you may never have heard of

People do what they are paid to. Management teams are people paid to govern the firm. Should we be interested in knowing how, why and when managers are paid? For this reason, some of the world's most influential investors say that Form DEF14A is foremost in understanding the valuation prospects of a company.

Companies with stocks which the public can buy and sell are required to file Form DEF14A every year. In this publicly available report, management is required to state how they are paid, how much they are paid, and their incentives for payment. Compensation plans drive management. Management drives the strategies of the firm.
What do investors discover by studying the DEF14A document? It's not surprising that management teams who aren't given the right incentives to create value *'don't create value.'*

Shareholder 'Activism'

The world's largest pension fund, the world's greatest private equity firms, and the world's best performing hedge funds know this rule well. By simply realigning management teams with basic wealth-creation rules, significant value can be unlocked or created. Without this alignment, many other business activities become immaterial to the firm's valuation.

The world's largest pension fund is CalPERs, a pension fund for California public employees. The fund is known for its 'shareholder activism.' The shareholder activism group focuses on whether or not management is aligned with the investors of the firm by their compensation, benefits, and other ways the firm is governed. CalPERs publicly engages the boards and management teams of companies in a number of ways to ensure that management's incentives are aligned with the investors.

Research in the 'Wilshire Study' by Wilshire Associates from 1987 to mid-2006 found that CalPERs' shareholder activism over the course of several years had helped those firms to improve such that their respective stock prices increased by hundreds of millions of dollars.

It's interesting to note that CalPERs was not advising on product launches, or on market segments, or any other areas of business traditionally thought of as 'strategy.' CalPERs focused on one main area, ensuring that the management team's compensation and benefits were creating incentives aligned with basic wealth-creation goals as discussed here. That alone allowed many other wealth-creating activities to occur. It's another explanation of why Tenet One, Ethically Maximize Wealth, is at the top of the pyramid as the first step in strategic analysis and business planning.

Concluding notes on Tenet One

The power remains with the people. Wealth cannot be maximized to investors, owners, or managers of a business by taking it from others. Wealth is created by placing the firm in a position to facilitate the activities of investors, customers, employees, and business partners as they exchange their time, money, or resources in return for the fulfillment of their needs. Flourishing economies have always been dependent on this concept. Businesses that act as central points of these exchanges are able to generate wealth for their owners over sustained durations.

The customers, employees, owners, and general public are the ones who grant a firm failure or success. The management team is only a vehicle for allowing that flow of success to happen – one representation of it is the flow of cash.

In the long-term, one can only maximize owner's wealth if society's wealth increases also, in a win-win-win situation for customers, employees, investors, and all involved. As with any democracy, the people who surround the business are responsible for its prosperity.

If the firm does well and the business is creating wealth *at its maximum potential*, it's merely a reflection of its positive – and non-negative – impact on the world.

Key Diagnostics for Tenet One

Has wealth been defined specifically with monetary and non-monetary objectives, timetables, and acceptable risk levels?

Can that definition of wealth be achieved without violating the ethical parameters of the communities in which the business operates (and hopes to operate)? Can management adequately understand and evaluate what its communities deem as unethical?

Does management have the internal controls, culture, and expectations in place which steward the business within the ethical parameters set by the business's communities?

Are management and the entire firm focused and aligned with maximizing investors' wealth as defined?

Does management understand the basic rules of monetary wealth-creation as cash flows would describe?

Does the business employ Genuine Assets to better assure achievement of Tenet One? Is a process in place for building these Genuine Assets?

Is management continually on the watch for and aware of forces of change that could limit the firm's ability to execute on Tenet One in the future?

Are the right metrics in place and reviewed regularly to help management monitor and communicate the business's ability to execute on Tenet One? Are monetary goals defined in terms of cash flows and cash flow potential?

Explanation of HOLT Relative Wealth Charts

These charts are used at the end of each chapter to bring the concepts alive and show their link to performance and valuation. A more detailed explanation is provided in the appendix.

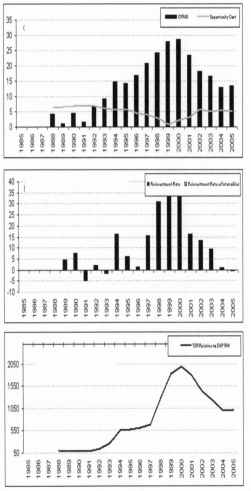

The top panel of the chart compares CFROI® level represented by the bars, to the Opportunity Cost of Capital, represented by the line, based on HOLT's calculations. An analogy would relate the CFROI measure to the interest paid by a savings account, while the cost of capital is related to an average bank interest rate. Rates higher than average are better. The comparison covers a history of the last 21 years.

The middle panel displays the reinvestment rate or growth in assets, represented by the bars. These should always be viewed in context of the CFROI levels in the top panel. In the savings account analogy, reinvestment rate is like an increase in prinicipal. If the interest rate is high, higher reinvestment rates create more value. If the interest rate is low, low or even negative investment is best.

The bottom panel displays annual changes in stock price valuation (including dividend payouts) relative to the return of a major stock market index, such as the S&P 500 in the USA. Stock price levels are driven by changing expectations of future CFROI returns and reinvestment rates. An upwardly sloping line is "beating the market." A downward sloping line is underperforming.

(This example features Nokia.)

Johnson & Johnson (JNJ)

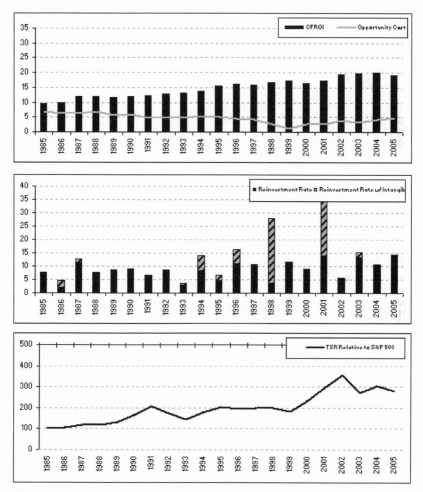

In an economic democracy, businesses succeed when they create offerings that answer the needs of the constituents: notably, the customers, employees, and investors. The JNJ credo specifically acknowledges all of the important aspects of Tenet One.

The firm has shown an ability to accomplish all the tenets of Return Driven Strategy. Their measure of "Capital Efficient Profitable Growth"(CEPG) is one compelling way of stating what is seen in the above chart. The firm shows two decades of improving CFROI levels on an increasing investment base. Together, these drive market outperformance.

Tyco International (TYC)

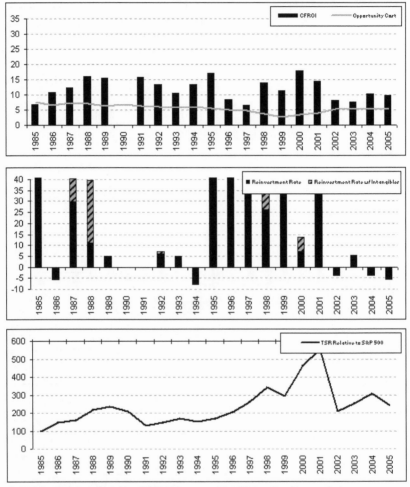

Despite an impressive track record of performance over a long period of time, in 2002 Tyco's management was found to have committed gross unethical conduct in a number of ways. Suddenly, the quality of the firm's offerings, the diligent work of its employees, and the loyalty of the customers could do little to stem the impact of the violations of Tenet One.

CFROI levels fell by half, and growth completely shut down. The firm's valuation fell by over *$100 billion dollars*. Five years later, returns, growth rates, and valuation levels remained relatively stagnant.

Enron (ENE)

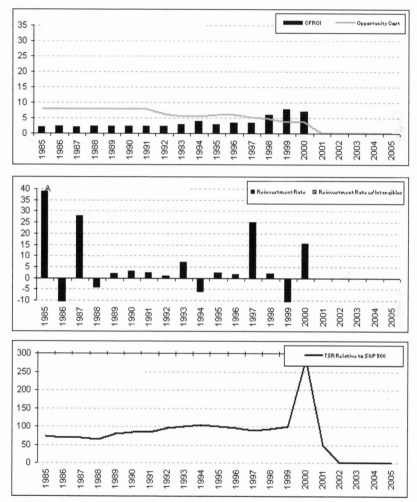

In 1998, 1999, and 2000, it would have appeared that Enron impressively lifted its CFROI plateau from below cost of capital to above. The firm was seen as a true innovator, and would have appeared to generate unbelievable cash flows. Unfortunately, the disregard for business ethics by Enron's management team resulted in bankruptcy.

The firm had previously been worth tens of billions of dollars. The team's gross unethical conduct was directed toward investors and employees in particular. How many thousands of jobs were lost because of the firm's actions? The impact of this behavior overwhelmed any other good qualities of the firm.

Xerox (XRX)

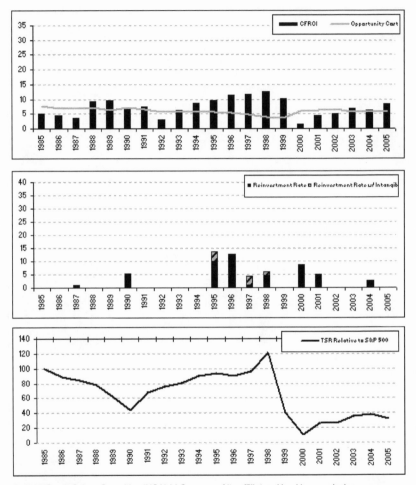

From 1997 to 2000, Xerox executives engaged in an accounting scheme that one regulator from the Securities and Exchange Commission claimed in 2002 was a 'pattern of pervasive fraud.' The firm's management committed gross unethical conduct by misrepresenting the company's performance in the billions of dollars.

The fall in stock price over two years was dramatic. Seven years later, the firm still hasn't been able to recover to the previous 20 year low point in valuation in 1990. Despite a brand that is a household name, extensive innovation, and other impressive assets, gross unethical conduct at Xerox has had the greatest impact on value creation.

Bethlehem Steel

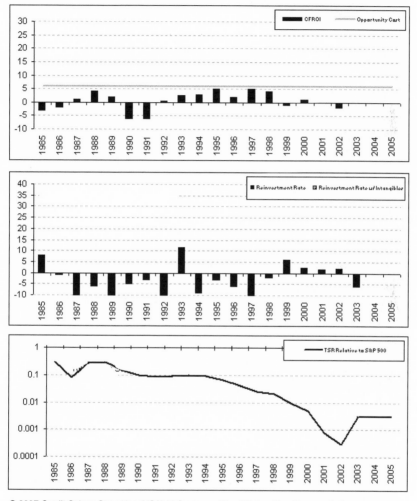

When firms destroy value for prolonged periods of time, they also hurt other areas of the economy. Lost jobs, wasted resources, and lost opportunities characterize a firm with CFROI levels that never exceed the cost of capital. The only recourse for a firm like this is to divest assets until it can at least reach a state of not destroying value.

In the last five years of this chart, Bethlehem Steel switched into a state of growing assets, putting more money to work at a rate of return barely above zero, if not below. Valuations collapsed even further.

Part Two

The Goal Tenets

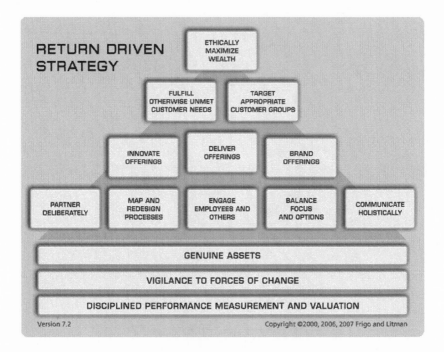

Tenet Two

Fulfill Otherwise Unmet Customer Needs

The path to the creation of wealth is through the customer, by fulfilling their unmet needs. This is the recipe for achieving high returns on investment. High-performance businesses deliver an offering which the customers believe is not otherwise available.

- Identify – and have a process for continually identifying – exactly what needs cause customers to buy what they buy

- Identify – and have a process for continually identifying – what customers would buy if it were available, but cannot. Thereby, an unmet need is identified

- Focus on the real reasons for purchase, and not simply functional attributes of goods or services, redefining terms such as 'quality' in light of the customer's perception of an offering's purpose

- Focus on how to move away from pricing goods and services based on internal costs. When possible, pricing should be based on the value the customer receives when no substitute is available

- Realize that competition or pricing wars do not come from an outside organization's attack, but on an internal inability to create offerings that fulfill customer needs uniquely

- Employ Genuine Assets to allow the firm to build and sustain unique capabilities in need identification and fulfillment, through customer relationships and intelligence

- Be vigilant to forces of change which affect customer needs, customer perceptions of their needs, and the ability to gather information about those needs. Adjust to these changes, even radically when necessary

- In performance measures, focus on the pricing power a firm enjoys relative to both the cost of the offerings AND the cost of assets required to produce those offerings

Can a great product or service really make for a great business?

Time and again, an assumption is raised in business analysis that great products will naturally lead to great profits and great businesses. Unfortunately, this is very often not the case.

The BMW 'great product' conundrum

BMW provides an incredibly 'high-end' offering, yet the BMW Company's profitability levels have been at corporate averages at best (so are Mercedes, and many other 'high-end' car manufacturers). BMW's slogan is 'the ultimate driving machine,' and with good reason. People who have had the pleasure of owning a 7-series have likely contemplated selling their house and moving into their car. The BMW 3-series consistently shows up at the top of the ranks for the most satisfying cars to own. The company often wins accolades such as 'Top Customer Satisfaction' from J.D. Power. So, why does BMW show cash flow returns that are average?

If we analyze their cash flow returns, we see a business that is not nearly as great as the product it provides. Until 2000, BMW did not produce returns equal to its cost of capital. How is it possible a producer of such a popular, high quality, high-priced product could be just an average company in cash flow returns?

A firm's cash flow return potential is controlled in part by the existence of substitutes. The impact of substitute offerings is a primary concern for business planning, and is the central point of 'Porter's Five Forces.' Michael Porter is one of the most frequently quoted authors on the subject of business strategy. He is heralded for his *Structural Analysis of Industries* and the famous five forces model that he developed.

Of those forces, the existence of substitute offerings implies that Tenet Two of Return Driven Strategy cannot be achieved. If two competing offerings are adequately available for fulfilling a particular need, then the need fulfilled by either of them is not *otherwise unmet*. For this reason, substitutes control a firm's pricing power, and thereby the creation and sustainability of its returns on investment.

Does this business produce an offering that fulfills the customer need without substitute, and if so, how long can that last?

As satisfied as customers may be with a product, a slightly cheaper replacement with similar utility will draw customers away. There is no question that BMW offers a 'high-end' product, but so do Mercedes-Benz, Audi, Lexus, and Cadillac. Because there are alternatives to BMWs, the Bavarian company has little pricing power, regardless of the value its customers receive from its offerings.

A company that does not have pricing power will never have sustainable, high cash flows. As long as suitable substitutes exist for fulfilling a particular customer need, customers will drive prices down to the costs to produce them. Contrast that with a situation when no substitutes are available and customers freely pay based on the value they receive. The difference in the impact on business performance can be enormous.

The difference between a great business and a business with great offerings is best summarized: Great products and services make customers happy and can generate high revenues. Great businesses sell offerings that customers need and without that offering, the customer's need would have gone unmet. They thereby generate not only high revenues, but also higher cash flow returns.

Billions sold...with average returns

Fulfilling great customer needs does not alone lead to profitable businesses. Along with air and water, we need food to live. Yet, groceries and restaurants are not necessarily businesses with the highest cash flow returns.

McDonald's has built a franchise the world over, with over 30,000 stores across the globe. The offering attracts a multitude of customers with revenues in the tens of billions.

To put McDonald's performance into perspective, from 1995-2000, the firm averaged more than four new store openings per day. Revenues increased significantly over 10 years. McDonald's clearly offers a product that people want. However, are these products without substitute?

Over the past two decades, McDonald's return on investment has been around 7%, or barely above long-term corporate averages. These levels fall far below what one might expect from an industry leader. The problem may be that the term 'industry leader' is often applied to firms with the highest sales or market share and not by the achievement of above-average returns on investment.

Plenty of substitutes prevent McDonald's from improving returns. The company is able to grow sales by increasing the volume of units sold, but the prices have not been sufficiently higher than the costs to produce the offerings. Too many other restaurants exist which customers would switch to if McDonald's attempted to raise prices.

Adequate availability of substitutes translates to lack of pricing power. Low pricing power means low returns, no matter how high sales growth can be.

Are the real needs the obvious ones?

Before the personal computer division was sold to Lenovo, IBM's ThinkPads had long been considered the better laptops on the market. They had been consistent front-runners in many awards for notebook quality and customer service. IBM desktops had also been considered innovative, high quality products. Yet, IBM had lost hundreds of millions on its personal computing division.

IBM was building high quality machines, but was this exactly what the market needed?

While IBM's PC business was suffering through ongoing losses, Dell was producing CFROI® levels in excess of 20%, dominating all other personal computer manufacturers in the United States. What was the reason for this incredible success in a time when other manufacturers like IBM were suffering?

Dell had been targeting a need that no other manufacturer had before – mass customization in a direct-to-customer model. Dell provided an approach to computer production and delivery that was truly unique at the time. The now famous Dell Direct model sought to fulfill the need of the customer for choice and flexibility in building exactly the machine the customer wanted. Something near impossible to do efficiently in the consumer channels where IBMs and other PCs were available.

Dell provided an offering for which there was no true substitute. It was able to produce amazingly high returns. It had created a situation where it did not have to price relative to its costs to produce. Avoiding cost-plus pricing and moving toward customer value-pricing is necessary for high cash flow returns.

Great offerings do not guarantee great results

Having a great existing product – or one on the horizon – is not reason enough for a company to be a great investment. Smart investors will examine whether or not management understands the true needs of the customer, and whether or not other means are available for fulfilling that need.

In general, certain needs are more important than others

People seem to be motivated differently by different kinds of need. By examining needs in terms of pain and pleasure, one can evaluate the value of an offering to the customer.

- Customers seem to apply highest value to offerings which reduce immediate perceived pains when no other pain-reducing options exist. They then pay prices relative to that value.

- Next, customers apply value to the potential of future pain, and again, the perception that no other offering will forestall that future pain.

- Lastly, customers seem to apply value to the potential for pleasure received.

Some of the firms with the highest revenues and cash flow returns are those which have created a series of offerings which have no substitute and target great pains being felt by the customer.

- Pharmaceutical and medical device companies such as Pfizer (PFE) and Medtronic (MDT) have provided treatments for immediate sicknesses and also the extension of life. The relief of the pains from sickness can command value-based prices and thereby generate high cash flow returns.

- Headhunting firms like Robert Half (RHI) have shown high cash flow returns as they provided jobs to people who either have no job, can't wait to leave their current one, or desire higher compensation or opportunities. For the employer, recruiting that relieves the pain a manager can have in not having the right employee, can be perceived to be an otherwise unmet need.

- Payroll servicing firms such as Paychex (PAYX) have allowed businesses to not be so bogged down with payroll and administrative functions which can take valuable time away from more important business activities. One of the largest complaints from managers of firms, particularly small ones, is the pain of not having 'enough time in the day.' If a servicing firm can uniquely help a manager gain an hour or two a day, the value is whatever the manager places on that time, which could be very high.

Being different is not core to strategy. It's a by-product

Being different for the sake of being different? Being different is not core to strategy, it's only a by-product of having done everything else right. The firm that fulfills *otherwise unmet* needs is naturally a different firm. The goal of being different for its own sake could lead to bankruptcy.

After all, it's better to be like everyone else and still be in business than to be different and be bankrupt. Survivorship bias can make someone believe the manager's statement to be true:

> *"Well, I'm not sure if we're going down the right path, but at least it's a different strategy from our competitors, and being different has got to be a good thing, right?"*

In other words, high return firms always offer a product or service which is different. High-performing firms have distinctly different strategies, however, many failed companies which have gone bankrupt also displayed uniqueness. For instance, consider the thousands of Internet start-ups that tried something very different. Better to be a commodity and survive than to be different and go broke.

The pack of average performers all seem to have commoditized, non-differentiated strategies. Therefore, it would appear that 'different is good.'

Apple has always been different

Throughout its life cycle, over 20 years or more, Apple Computer's products have always been renowned for being different. Yet, the firm has displayed a roller coaster of results through that period, beginning high, falling dramatically, and then rising again in recent years.

The firm has shown many ways of being different:

- As a philosophical approach to being different, the company's powerful advertising campaigns have won awards for Apple's attempts to show uniqueness over the last ten to twenty years

- Being different and succeeding, as with the iPod, where competitor music players exist, but none so easy to use and garnering such attention

- Being different and nearly going broke, as with many of the Apple personal computer systems. Despite receiving the highest rewards of 'customer satisfaction,' many of these systems simply had too few customers wishing to satisfy their computing needs with Apple's products during the 1990s

'Different' is a natural state of successful, high-performers, but should never be the goal in and of itself. Better to focus on customer needs, fulfilling them in unique ways, as the state of being different naturally occurs.

Pricing competition is a reflection of an internal weakness

"We are under significant pricing pressure from competitors."

Despite this commonly-made statement, pricing pressure comes from the customer, not from competitors. Weaker-than-desired performance does not stem from some outside competitive force; it comes directly from an inability to fulfill customer needs.

Again, it's not another company which creates pricing pressure; it's the customer... and a failure of the business to provide the customer something they really need which they can't get elsewhere. The beauty of 'price' is in what it communicates about need and its fulfillment by a business.

The real source of competition

For lower performing firms to improve their returns, the organization needs to be empowered to focus and frame the right problem. This requires owning up to the responsibility for the source of competition.

An inaccurate view of competitive strategy has created a major gap in understanding how to succeed. The very belief that *your competition does something to you* is the thinking which accompanies poor cash flows. It is not the competition that withholds cash flows from a business; it is the customers or potential customers.

The toy retailer, Toys R Us, displayed poor and declining returns for several years. Once the top toy retailer in the US, it has been surpassed by Wal-Mart. However, Wal-Mart isn't the source of Toys R Us's problems.

Toys R Us achieves below-average returns. It hasn't been able to create a unique offering for fulfilling the real needs of its potential customers – that justifies its investments in assets. The toy company openly stated that its strategy included competing with the 'broadest range of merchandise.' Wal-Mart probably does not have even a third of the in-store range of toy merchandise. Yet it has become the number one seller of toys.

The problem lies in the strategy. In the age of the Internet, competing with broadest selection or obscure items is best done through the World Wide Web. For the physical stores, something else should be the focus of answering the customer needs. Putting blame in the right place empowers a firm for building a better strategy. Awareness of the real problem is the first step.

How Wal-Mart (WMT) has pricing power

How can WMT have pricing power when their goods are the least expensive? Because those 'always low' prices are still far higher than the costs of making those goods available to the public.

In effect, WMT is able to price way above their costs; not necessarily the cost of goods sold but above the cost of the assets required to sell them: the warehouses, trucks, equipment, and other assets.

Even though their prices are lower than others, they're still able to price sufficiently high so as to generate returns more than double their cost of capital, for decades. In other words...WMT has the ability to price their goods far more cheaply and still generate higher returns.

The amazing thing is that Wal-Mart's prices could even be cheaper still and the firm could still generate a handy profit. But, they don't have to price more cheaply than they already are... because customers are already flocking to the Wal-Mart stores in droves. Wal-Mart only has to be cheaper than everyone else to fulfill the customers' unmet needs.

Wal-Mart is not a cost-plus pricer. It sets prices based on customer need and the value to the customer, and not based on its costs to produce. If it priced its goods based on its costs, their goods would be even less expensive than they are now.

Without any sophisticated analysis, a business can learn whether or not it is fulfilling an otherwise unmet need. The question a manager should ask is, "Does it seem like the firm can price its offerings based on the value to the customer, or does it price on some competitive margin over and above its costs to produce them?" The former is preferred over the latter, and necessary to generating high cash flow returns.

Pricing power from scope

The retail banking space is extremely competitive and most products like checking accounts, savings accounts, and CDs appear to have little differentiation.

Yet, throughout the 1990s and into the 21st Century, Wells Fargo bank has displayed returns on investment that are two or three times corporate averages. They have also shown extraordinary growth rates and a stock price that has increased 4 or 5 times that of the US market over the last 20 years.

To generate high returns, a firm must answer an unmet need. How is that accomplished when the product's offering has little functional differentiation? There may be something other than the obvious functional aspects of the product. The delivery of the product needs to be considered the offering as well. Wells Fargo has sought to create a one-stop shop for retail banking customers. The idea is to save them time while also reducing the firm's costs to market to them.

Dick Kovacevich, CEO at Wells Fargo, explained their performance in an interview in USA Today,

> *"We're really selling commodity products."* But, he adds, *"It's the way you distribute the commodity products that make it unique. What we're able to do with cross-selling is make banking much more convenient. It's also less expensive."*

A focus on timing and convenience of the customer seems to have paid off. The average Wells Fargo customer household uses 5.2 different bank products, about twice the industry average, and 20% of customers buy eight products from the bank.

This highlights how pricing power needs to be examined not only for the price above the cost of the offering itself, but also relative to the investments and other expenses required to build the business. In Wells Fargo's case, the cost is reduced through the one-stop shop. The result is a higher return on investment for the firm, while the customer's need for time and convenience is better fulfilled.

Competitive strategy redefined

The problem with competitiveness lies in a tendency toward competition for competition's sake. This is exasperated when a company does something simply because its competitors have begun doing it.

High-performance firms focus on the customer need and remain open to anything the business could create to uniquely fulfill it. Low return firms spend the balance of their time focusing on what the supposed competition is doing – and what has to be done to keep up with them. That's a sure-fire way to ensure mediocrity over time. Businesses that redefine them around the customer need are able to sustain high returns over time.

Truly being competitive

The greatest sales strategy techniques are actually 'needs-identification' techniques. Colgate-Palmolive has had significantly high cash flow returns over two decades. With good reason, as they claim they have over 50 million customer research touch-points every year, and innovate their offerings based on that.

The key is in having a deep commitment to making a difference in customer's lives, not just satisfying a particular task or function. High-performance firms understand customer needs at a very deep level. In other words, the diagnosis of the customer pain is the most important part of selling. The presentation and 'sale' of the appropriate medicine to cure that pain is relatively easy if the diagnosis is correct, and immaterial if the diagnosis is faulty or nonexistent.

How surveys can steer the strategy wrong

Customer satisfaction surveys are not a dependable way for driving to be a great business. First, it's hard to imagine a customer who would have said any of the following in a customer satisfaction survey:

> *"I need a retailer that drives efficiencies from its supplier base… and passes on the savings to me."*

"I need a payroll company which hires specifically from community colleges."

"I need the world wide web."

Yet each of these statements would have led to what we have seen as great businesses in Wal-Mart, Paychex, and many Internet firms. There are many other creative ways of discovering what it is that clients need, but would not necessarily come from a survey. The following are just a few:

- Customer interviews, phone-based and face-to-face
- Focus groups
- 'Day-in-the-Life' research
- Actual usage observation studies
- Studying the customers' customers, and even *their* customers
- 'Why-Axis' analysis: keep asking 'why' a customer behaves a certain way, until the question can't be asked anymore

Abraham Maslow and business strategy

In any customer research, Maslow's Hierarchy can be a valuable tool for identifying innate levels of need. Abraham Maslow is studied in most courses on basic psychology. He identified a set of needs that all humans have innately.

- Physiological needs, such as food and water
- Safety and security
- Community and belonging
- Self-esteem
- Self-actualization

One level must be transcended before a higher level can be reached. In Maslow's model, a person cannot pursue their need for community or belonging if they are malnourished or lack shelter. When a person's need for community and belonging are adequately fulfilled, he or she then has the potential for reaching a level of self-esteem.

So, does a person purchase a particular can of soda because it quenches thirst, or because of some other need fulfilled? Does a customer choose a vehicle based on the transportation – or the self-esteem the car provides? For different customers, different needs are fulfilled.

An extensive repertoire of customer research and need techniques are necessary because of the frequency with which businesses misjudge what the real needs are and the real reasons customers buy.

The path is not the destination

Tenet Two must never violate Tenet One. In the pursuit of need fulfillment, society's need for ethical business practices cannot be ignored. In determining which needs to pursue, investors' definition of wealth should remain the end-goal. Meanwhile, Tenet Two is an umbrella tenet to all the lower-placed tenets in the pyramid.

Concluding notes on Tenet Two

A beautiful economic system is one where higher profitability is rewarded to firms that find ways to uniquely respond to and fulfill the needs of society. The firms which have created most notably high levels of wealth are driven by people who wake up every morning thinking about the plight of others, the needs of others, and specifically the otherwise unmet needs of others.

Instead of going through the day thinking, "how do I make more money today?" the successful leader knows that the following thinking will naturally lead to wealth creation:

> *"What is it that people really need, that they don't get fulfilled, and how can I find a way to provide for it?"*

High-performance business managers do not dwell so much on wealth itself, but set their intention for wealth at the outset, and then focus squarely on the customer.

Businesses which succeed redefine competitive analysis along the lines of these tenets, and not competition for competition's sake. These firms align their organizations along customer needs, not just along product lines, and certainly not along a seemingly arbitrary definition of 'industry.'

Real social good comes from a wealth-creating firm. The proof that a firm has succeeded is not based on imagined goodwill or hope, but on the distinctly measurable fact that people are willing to pay for offerings in ways that result in a greatly profitable business. That financial state is merely society's reward to the business for fulfilling its unmet needs.

Key Diagnostics for Tenet Two

Does the business have a process in place for continually researching, understanding, and describing the current and future unmet needs of customers?

Does the business produce offerings which fulfill customer needs in ways which no one else can, evident by a value-pricing capability and returns above averages?

Does the business define competitive analysis around customer need fulfillment – and not simply around traditional competitor analysis?

Is the business able to price offerings relative to the value of the good to the customer, or based on some margin above the costs to produce?

Does management create an environment such that the business's customer research and need fulfillment are consistent with and do not violate the first tenet?

Does the business employ Genuine Assets to better assure achievement of this tenet? Is a process is in place for building these Genuine Assets?

Is management continually on the watch for and aware of significant forces of change which could limit the firm's ability to execute on Tenet Two in the future?

Are the right metrics in place and reviewed regularly to help management monitor and communicate the business's ability to execute on Tenet Two?

Wal-Mart Stores (WMT)

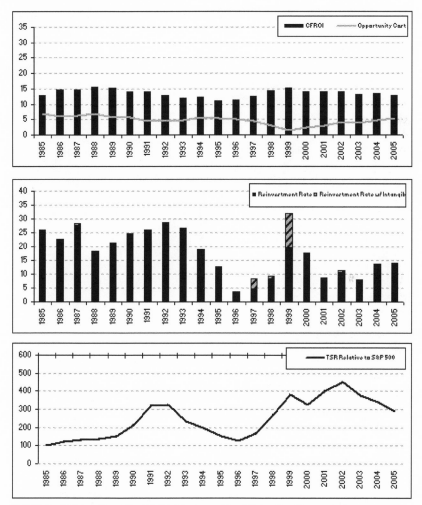

Wal-Mart has built unique processes and relationships such that it can offer household goods at prices that are lower than most any other retailer can match. The firm's pricing power comes not from its ability to charge high prices relative to the costs of goods, but that it has such low levels of investment required to produce such high levels of sales. The firm has continually expanded its ability to fulfill more and more needs.

For over twenty years, Wal-Mart's CFROI levels exceed double the cost of capital and high growth rates have delivered a phenomenal valuation. Note in the bottom panel that great companies are not always great stocks. Valuations are driven by expectations of performance which are influenced by, but necessarily equal to, posted performance.

Kimberly-Clark Corp (KMB)

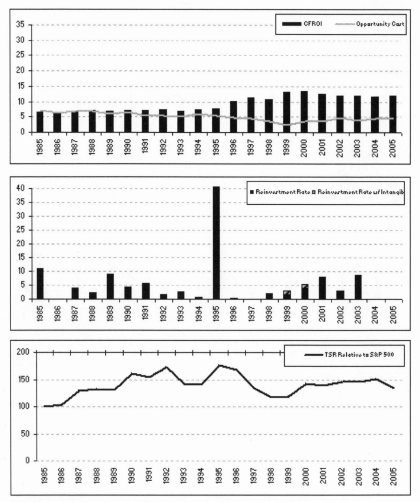

Once mainly a supplier of commoditized paper, Kimberly-Clark has not fallen in performance like other paper firms around the world. Over two decades, the firm has progressively moved into high-return businesses such as consumer products. KMB's consumer offerings can be branded and innovated in ways such that consumers perceive the products to fulfill needs that are otherwise unmet, particularly relative to plain paper products.

KMB's CFROI levels have increased steadily, with reasonable growth rates, and a stock price that has kept up with market averages and beyond. Many other "paper "companies have not shown such solid performance.

Wells Fargo (WFC)

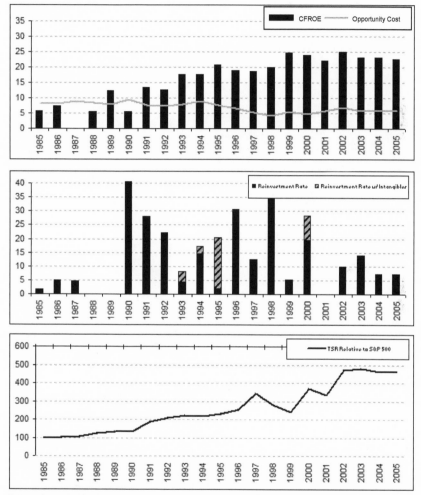

As the CEO of Wells Fargo has described, individual banking products could be commoditized, but the grouping, marketing, delivery, and packaging of them can make for a unique offering, answering customers' needs of convenience and saving time. This drives high CFROE levels.

From 1985 to 1995, Wells Fargo was able to grow its equity base while increasing its performance. In the latter years of the chart, CFROE levels are high, but not higher, and growth rates slow down. During that time, valuations follow suit. (Financial services firms are measured on a CFROE measure instead of CFROI.)

BMW (BMWG)

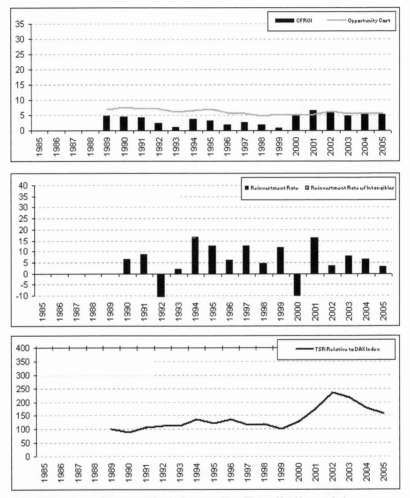

The difference between a great product and a great business is evident in the cash flows. Regardless of how luxurious a BMW vehicle may be, in order to generate pricing power, there must be no substitute. While some customers certainly believe BMW is unique, not enough of these customers have existed that would pay high enough prices for BMW to generate above average returns.

However, as the CFROI levels shift in 2000 from 'poor' returns to 'average' returns, the firm's stock price moves markedly upward. A great stock and a great company are not always the same thing. Change in performance expectations drives change in valuation levels, not necessarily the level of performance posted.

McDonald's (MCD)

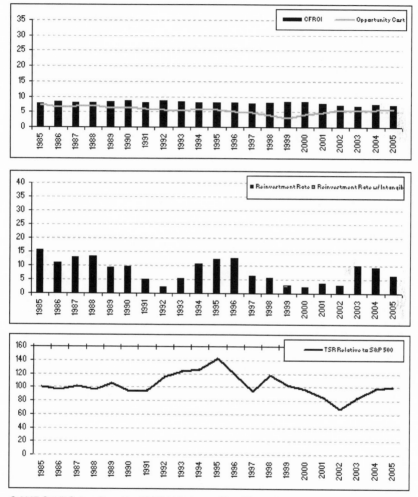

Corporate average CFROI levels in the United States have been around 6% for the last 20 or more years. McDonald's has shown an ability to generate CFROI returns only slightly above that long-term average. Yet, McDonald's has billions and billions of repeat sales, and has grown stores in the thousands. The ability to grow is not necessarily representative of the fulfillment of an otherwise unmet need.

When CFROI levels are around the cost of capital, the value of asset growth is questionable. When this occurs, changes in returns, and not growth, become the primary driver for a stock price.

Apple (AAPL)

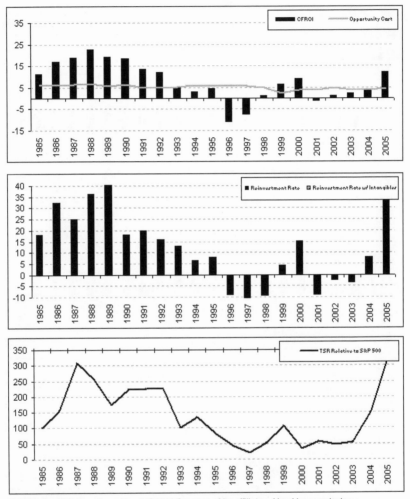

Being different is not core to strategy, it's merely a by-product when unique offerings fulfill otherwise unmet needs. Over the last two decades, Apple has shown the extremes of being different, always with unique offerings, but not always generating high performance levels.

From 1990 to 1995, Apple grew a business with falling CFROI levels and a sharply declining stock price. From 1995 to 2003, the reduction of poor-performing assets maintains valuation levels. Most recently, with the advent of the iPod, high growth and high CFROI returns drive higher stock prices.

Southwest (LUV)

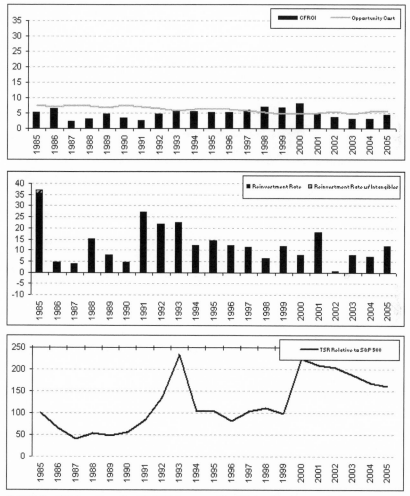

With such incredible popularity with customers and the financial press, Southwest Airlines is an example of a business with great products that has not yet become a great business. CFROI levels have seldom reached corporate averages and the firm enjoys little if any pricing power.

The fact that the firm is one of the best in its industry is commendable, but over the long haul, investment performance has only been slightly above average. The years of the firm's best stock performance have more to do with the low expectation levels set earlier. LUV's valuations marginally exceed the cost of the assets put in place, as the low CFROI returns would suggest.

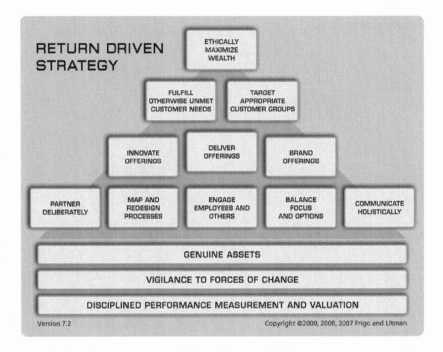

Tenet Three

Target Appropriate Customer Groups

This is the partner tenet to Tenet Two. If the path to high returns is through the customer, then the path to wealth-creation is through targeting lots and lots of customers.

- Group potential customers based on the characteristics of Tenet Two with descriptive traits which identify similar unmet needs

- Identify groups where there is higher potential for the business to provide unique offerings to fulfill those needs

- Target customer groups whose size, growth rates, and potential changes support the creation of wealth as it has been defined

- Target customer groups whose needs are large enough to justify the upfront and ongoing investments required to create and deliver the right offerings

- Target 'actionable' customer groups where the firm has the potential to be the dominant provider of unique offerings which fulfill otherwise unmet needs

- Recognize how being the dominant provider to any particular customer group sets the stage for high returns, but still requires achievement of Tenet Two

- Employ Genuine Assets which allow the firm to target appropriately large or growing markets with efficiencies and advantages which other firms cannot replicate

- Be vigilant to forces of change which continually affect customer groupings, the traits for defining those groups, and the choices over which groups to target, as well as other aspects of this tenet. Adjust to these changes, even radically when necessary

- In performance measurement, include a focus on the size and growth rates of customer groups and how that will directly impact the required levels of resources of time and money and the opportunity for further investments of resources

Moving beyond industry woes

"It's not our fault."

Managers of poor-performing firms can be sometimes be heard to blame their woes on industry issues, poor cycles, or other unforeseen market occurrences beyond their control.

"We are suffering from a down-cycle in our industry."

In the face of troubling industry trends, management will naturally buckle down and focus on cost controls, lean manufacturing initiatives, and other forms of operational efficiencies. The hope is to wait out the poor cycle and contain costs as much as possible. However, many industries do not recover from down cycles *because they're not cycles at all.*

The following two extremes highlight how a manager could explain the company's poor performance in a troubled industry:

"It was a tough economic environment. Sales declined as our business fell with that environment."

Perennially poor-performing firms tend to speak in a blaming and even finger-pointing fashion. Blame is a convenient way of placing the responsibility for failure elsewhere, which may make the ego feel good in the short-run, but does not adequately prepare the firm for the future. Blaming performance on external forces reduces the manager's ability to take control.

In contrast, the following statement can be one of empowerment, as it points out things that could have been done, and could be done better in the future:

> *"Our performance suffered because we did not have the systems in place to notice the declining trends, and we were unable to act quickly enough to navigate around them."*

This may not be a statement made on a public conference call, but it may be one that resounds strongly internally. High-performing managers speak in ways that lean the firm toward potential actions, as opposed to helpless states. When the responsibility is brought home, the manager is empowered to make changes that could possibly avoid another failure, or better yet, take advantage of new opportunities.

Accepting responsibility over targeted customer groups

> *"I'm the best in a bad industry. Doesn't that count for something?"*

One way which businesses fulfill the needs of society is by producing offerings more efficiently – *'productive efficiencies.'* However, another way which businesses succeed is by knowing what goods or services should not be developed in the first place. Businesses succeed when managers know which industries to allocate resources and which ones not to – *'allocative efficiency.'*

Targeting the right markets is a key aspect of allocative efficiency, the third tenet of Return Driven Strategy. Getting out of the wrong industry is as important, and sometimes more so, than trying to stick it out to be the best of a bad industry. It's a sobering experience for a manager to realize that the source of performance woes has never been the industry at all, but the inability to target the right one in the first place.

From paper to something else

International Paper (IP) has exhibited consistently poor-performing cash flow returns over two or more decades. This reflects an environment where any pricing power is difficult to attain. In the annual report, the firm states that demand for their products *"is affected by general economic conditions."* No doubt the industry of commoditized paper supply is a tough one. Warren Buffett drives home a point consistent with Tenet Three of Return Driven Strategy: *"When management with a reputation for brilliance tackles a business with a reputation for poor fundamentals, it is the reputation of the business that remains intact."*

However, product demand is also based on producing the right offerings for the right markets. Kimberly-Clark, also a player in the paper industry, saw the issues with that industry and had to recognize that consumer products businesses flourished with much higher high cash flow returns than those in simply paper production.

People may not realize today just how much KMB used to be a paper company like International Paper. Over the last ten or more years, however, the difference in their cash flow generating abilities is remarkable. As KMB moved into the consumer products space with well-known products like Kleenex tissue paper, higher returns flowed with their decisions.

Another paper company, albeit years ago, was Nokia, the current telecom giant. The company shifted from being a paper company in a poor industry to many other things. Most notably for Nokia, they targeted telecom equipment. Their moves focused on high return industries over low return ones. Their efforts and resources moved consistently with that knowledge.

Managers in poor-performing industries will often cite the industry as the problem. However, as the paper company examples show, firms are seldom stuck within an industry. To perform well, business managers need to choose the right industry, and change industries when necessary. The managers might not control the industry's economics, but they can certainly control whether or not to be in that industry in the first place.

Shrink and grow rich?

"Our shareholders demand growth. We need to provide that."

"We must grow or we will die."

While many management teams will make these statements, they simply aren't true. Investors regularly attribute higher valuations to firms that have shown the fortitude to shrink a bad business.

Investors demand growth when it can generate high cash flow returns. They specifically demand 'shrink' when returns would appear otherwise. This is the way Tenets Two and Three are combined. How can we translate these financial concepts into a qualitative understanding?

Basic Guidelines of Wealth-Creation

- Grow the business when cash returns are above average business returns
- Shrink when cash returns are already below or expected to be below averages

These wealth-creation rules are violated regularly, as the following statements suggest:

"We're clearly the industry leader, but the market doesn't get it."

"We're a great company. We have over ten billion in revenues."

Growth is only valuable when profitability levels are above the levels which investments could have generated elsewhere, above the opportunity costs.

Group customers with "like need" in an actionable manner

Customers could be grouped geographically or demographically, such as targeting 'the Southeast US' or 'college students.' Some of the best characteristics for grouping customers appear to be those that are psychographics, 'characteristics of what or how people think.'

The best customer groupings allow the business to target the group with specific offerings based on similar needs among the group. High-performance firms specifically move business offerings toward market segments with the most appropriate size and growth potential, given the existence of unmet needs.

Be number 1 or 2 or get out

This statement highlights the importance of being a dominant player in an industry. In other words, it signifies the importance of being "the dominant fulfiller" of the needs of a group of customers. A statement to the effect of, "Be number 1 or 2 or get out," has been popularized by General Electric as a key to sustaining tremendous return levels. Many other firms plan and act with that mantra of being first or second – or consider exiting the industry. Several other high cash flow return businesses openly state the same thing, notably Kimberly-Clark and Colgate-Palmolive.

When margins are there, but profitability is not

Wealth-creating firms have a realistic understanding that enough customers must exist, with a deep enough unfulfilled need, to justify the upfront investment to create and deliver the offering in the first place.

Market size matters. A firm can enjoy pricing premiums relative to the cost of goods sold, but fail to sell enough goods at that price to cover the cost of investment. It is possible to have the "best" product, and yet still retain very low market share, as Apple computers experienced throughout the 1990s, with many years of negative cash flows.

A simple rule shines forth. Once appropriate market segments are targeted, corporate actions should seek to dominate those segments. And only segments that can reasonably be dominated should be targeted in the first place.

The difference between a monopoly and monopolization

Procter and Gamble purchased the Gillette Company in 2006. Prior to that, Gillette was a separate, publicly-traded company (Formerly ticker: G) with extremely high ROI levels.

One could argue that Gillette had certainly fulfilled otherwise unmet customer needs. People pay higher prices for Gillette's Mach 3 and Fusion razor blades because they see no real substitute in that particular segment. As discussed, it isn't enough that an offering is enjoyed and appreciated by customers. In order to achieve pricing power and the opportunity for higher returns, the product or service must be the only one which provides that particular enjoyment or need fulfillment. Gillette experienced amazingly high cash flow returns for years.

Gillette also strived to have product dominance on a category-by-category basis, effectively creating monopolies in the areas in which it competed. These economic monopolies are created by the uniqueness of the offerings and by customers freely choosing those products over others. The company followed Tenets Two and Three very well, with one exception… even dominance is not enough.

Shouldn't a monopoly be a great investment? Wouldn't an investor snatch up the chance to own part of a business with so many offerings which lack substitutes? The research shows that, despite monopoly-like cash flow returns to the company, Gillette's stock price still dropped precipitously from 1996 to 2000. Prior to being purchased by PG, Gillette's stock price still hadn't recovered to make up for it, even after several years.

Meanwhile, Wal-Mart has been a company which has created a business drawing consumers at amazing growth rates for decades. Its cash flow returns are high, as one might expect.

The firm also experienced enviable growth. Wal-Mart didn't merely create dominance in one category. The company succeeded in providing offerings in terms of price and convenience which have no adequate substitutes. More importantly, Wal-Mart has been able to repeat this in category after category – from toys to jewelry to groceries and many others. On top of that, the company continued to grow in the number of stores, square footage, and geographic region.

Wal-Mart achieved both high returns and high reinvestment rates. This powerful one-two combination, together with its exceptional stock price performance, supports the idea that monopolies do not maximize wealth. Monopolization is necessary.

It's easier to ride a wave than storm a beachhead

Bigger rewards can come to those firms which solve the needs of bigger numbers of customers. Firms that fight over customers whose needs are already serviced will always see relatively lower profits. Targeting large groups of underserved customers is an easier path to high returns.

Concluding notes on Tenet Three

The needs of society are not small. The world is an environment of scarce resources and growing populations with growing expectations. The larger the segment with a larger set of otherwise unmet needs, the more potential for wealth-creation.

The key to long-term wealth-creation is the fulfillment of great unmet needs of a great many people. Taking responsibility for the results being experienced today creates an empowering sense over the results to be created in the future.

With these intentions in mind, the manager can be ethically committed to wealth-creation, and drive positive changes into the business and society as a whole.

Key Diagnostics for Tenet Three

Does the business understand the existing and potential customer groups, identifying them based on characteristics that allow for actions toward fulfillment of their needs?

Do targeted customer groups have the market size potential – either through penetration of market share or future growth – which support resources required to generate returns and growth rates consistent with the defined goals of wealth-creation for the firm?

Does management target specific customer groups which can be dominated, where the firm is the number one or two provider for those needs?

Does management approach the above while functioning within the guidelines of Tenets One and Two?

Does the business use Genuine Assets to better assure achievement of this tenet? Is a process in place for building these Genuine Assets?

Is management continually on the watch for and aware of significant forces of change which could limit the firm's ability to execute on Tenet Three in the future?

Are the right metrics in place and reviewed regularly to help management monitor and communicate the business's ability to execute on Tenet Three?

Microsoft Corp (MSFT)

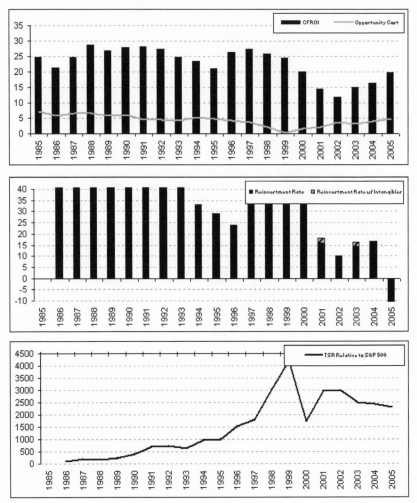

Microsoft's incredible valuations drove the stock price to increase at a whopping 25 times the rest of the stock market over the last 20 years. Such incredible performance cannot be driven by CFROI levels alone. Dominating application after successive application, the firm's growth rates created a compounding cash flow effect of a firm that continually monopolizes.

When the *monopolization* falls off after the 1990s, the *existing monopolies* can support the valuation level, but not increase it.

International Business Machines (IBM)

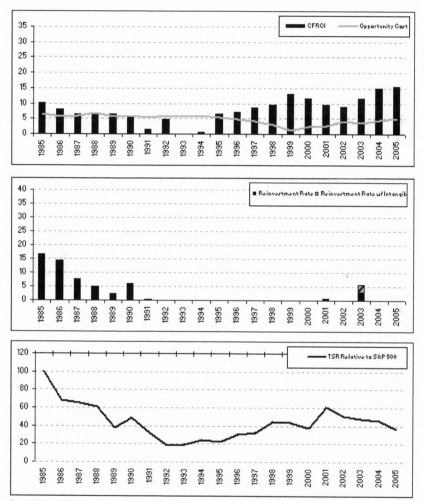

IBM's 20 years display the importance of examining the context of CFROI levels and growth rates together. High asset growth rates in the 1980s were accompanied by falling, low CFROI returns. Valuation levels fell dramatically. From 1985 to 1993, the stock returned 80% less than the stock market's average.

As poor assets were divested and CFROI levels improved dramatically from 1993 to 2005, the stock price also improved. However, it still hasn't recovered even half of the value it lost previously. Without the compounding value of asset growth with high returns, valuation levels stagnate.

HSBC (5)

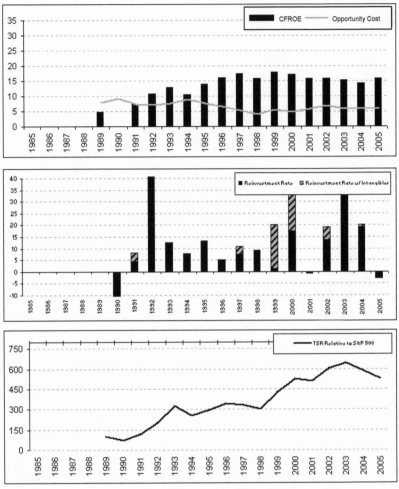

With the incredibly high growth rates of Asian countries, emerging markets, and global trade, a strategy focused on providing banking needs to a global community is a sound one. HSBC, from the name Hongkong and Shanghai Banking Corporation, displayed CFROE levels that increased steadily from 1990 to 1999, and have remained at least double the cost of capital since. High growth rates came from a global acquisition and organic growth, now with over 10,000 offices in 82 countries.

When high returns are coupled with high growth rates, the compounding effect takes hold, and valuations can skyrocket, as they have for HSBC.

Eastman Kodak (EK)

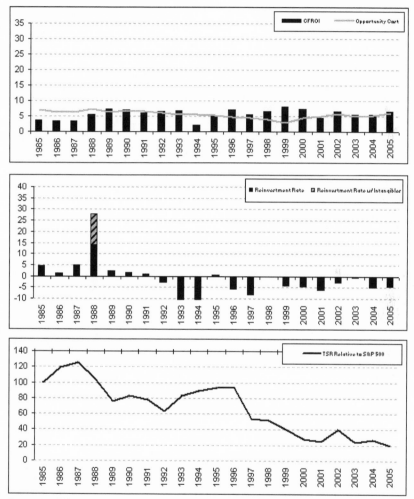

When faced with falling returns, Eastman Kodak has correctly focused on divesting assets. From 1990 to 2006, EK shed itself of 40% of its asset base in an attempt to keep CFROI levels from falling into negative territory.

Unfortunately, the firm generating a CFROI level of 6% to 7% on $20 billion of investment in 2006 is far less valuable than when it generated 6% to 7% on $38 billion of investment in 1990. While it may be the right thing to do to keep from something worse happening, the stock price still reflects a much, much lower valuation.

International Paper (IP)

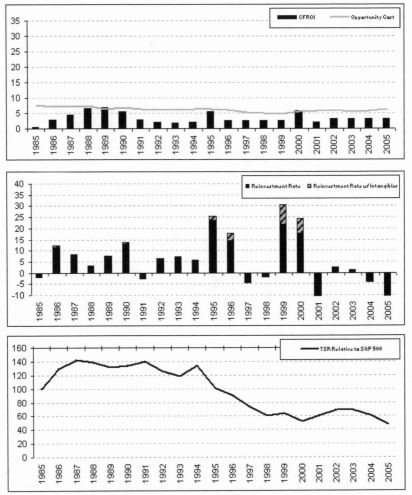

Growing a bad business is bad for the business. From 1985 to 2000, International Paper's' revenues increased by six times or about $24 billion dollars. However, during that time period, CFROI levels almost never broke through its opportunity cost of capital.

In such commoditized markets, the offering cannot be configured to fulfill an otherwise unmet need. Without Tenet Two, there is no pricing power. Without pricing power, low CFROI returns result, and growth is actually destructive to the value of the firm. The stock price underperformed the market greatly.

Infosys Technologies Limited (INFY)

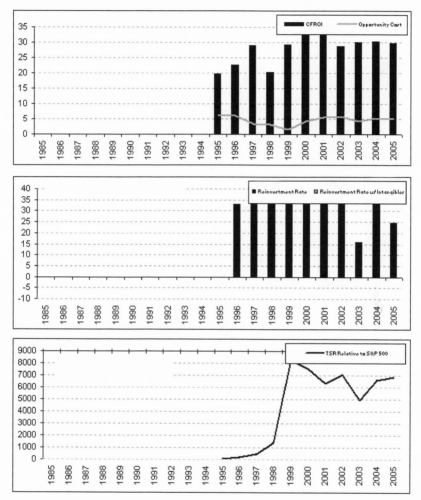

Few CFROI return and growth histories appear so high for a decade straight. While other technology firms fell when the tech bubble fell, Infosys focused on one area that continued to grow: strategic outsourcing.

As demands for Information Technology consulting and services increased globally, Infosys positioned itself, in India, to be able to service those demands and employing nearly 70,000 people, effectively and efficiently as the high CFROI pattern shows. The firm's value reached well over $20 billion in market capitalization. High growth rates come from targeting high growth customer groups of a particular customer need.

Part Three

The Competency Tenets

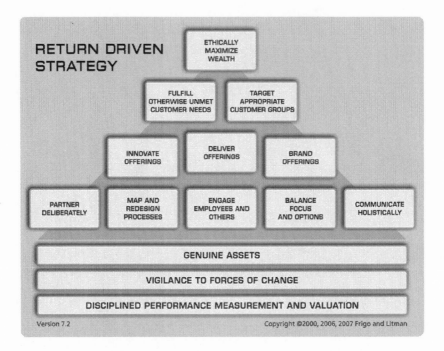

Tenet Four

Deliver Offerings

Tenet Four is the first of the three 'Competency Tenets' of a Return-Driven organization. The competencies describe the core functions of a business which are necessary to provide offerings which can fulfill the unmet needs of appropriately targeted customer groups.

This tenet, 'Deliver Offerings,' speaks to the effectiveness of the firm in providing the goods, services, and intangibles to achieve the higher three tenets.

- Recognize that the path to the fulfillment of customers' needs is through an offering: a combination of the physical and psychological attributes of what is being offered to a customer to fulfill their needs

- Provide offerings which perform the functions for customers as planned and promised, but most important, *at least as they expect*

- Consider a step between planning and implementation where the *executability* of a particular plan is questioned and tested

- Employ Genuine Assets which allow the firm to operate effectively and efficiently in ways which other firms cannot, when measured by the ability to produce and deliver offerings which achieve the higher tenets

- Be vigilant to forces of change which continually affect how the firm produces and delivers its offerings, as well as the nature of the offering itself, and adjust to these changes, even radically when necessary

- In performance measurement, include a focus on the size and growth rates of customer groups and how that will directly impact the required levels of resources of time and money and the opportunity for further investments of resources

Strategy... or the implementation of strategy?

Which is more important to business success, planning or the implementation of plans? This ongoing debate among management and strategy pundits has evolved into entire books targeting the subject. Lately, the trend appears to be toward the importance of implementation as in the popularized statement,

"It's the execution that matters."

However, the question as to which is more important, strategy or execution, is moot. How successful could a business possibly be if it executes well on an incredibly poor strategy? Certainly, great implementation of a bad plan could be just as troubling as poor implementation of a good one.

Instead, high-performing firms see strategy and execution as simply different focal points in the planning and action of achieving the higher tenets. The important question to ask is whether implementation activities are adequately aligned with planning activities, in the right ways and at the right times.

An unnecessary debate

"Anyone can come up with an idea, but it's the execution that really matters."

This quote highlights the importance of ideas and action together. Unfortunately, the statement can be taken to extremes, implying that the creation of a plan and the implementation of a plan are distinctly separate components. To believe that great businesses simply develop a strategy and then proceed to execute on it is folly. It is as if there were a 'step 1' and 'step 2'.

The impression that strategy and execution occur in a linear fashion like 'cause-and-effect' is misguided. Firms with mediocre or poor results appear to share a common thinking that businesses first strategize, and then follow and execute on the strategies. It would seem to make sense that first one plans, then one implements.

> *"At our annual company retreat we defined our five-year plan."*

The problem lies in the timing of planning and implementation. Given the rate of changing business environments, how much confidence could one have in executing on a strategy created years ago? High performance firms may set out on particular strategies, but are fully prepared to change them. In other words, strategy must be continually evaluated and adjusted based on the information coming from the implementation of the strategy.

Firms exhibiting high returns have a different planning culture in place. Strategic planning occurs on an ongoing basis as soon as new information and analysis suggest. As the business executes on its plans, managers gain new information. That information is then fed back into the planning process for reconsideration, immediately. This leads to avoidance of risks and capitalization of opportunities ahead of other firms.

Conceptually, it's easy to separate strategic planning from implementation. In reality, though, the lines should be blurred. Successful business plan execution produces the elements for successful planning for the future, and vice versa.

Offerings as the path to fulfillment

An offering is the total of the product, service, function, benefit, and psychological value that is designed by the firm to fulfill the needs of the customer. The concept should not be limited to the concepts of product and service, but to the entirety of the impact that the business can deliver to the customer.

The Goal Tenets, Tenets Two and Three, cite that the path to wealth-creation is through the customer, lots and lots of customers. Specifically, success is won by fulfilling the customers' unmet needs. It follows that the path to customer need fulfillment is through the design and development of the right offerings.

Strategy and execution, a continuum in sales

To sell an offering, a good salesperson knows the importance of actively listening to the customer. The ideal salesperson listens to the customer's needs, complaints, and pains. With that information, the business can provide the right offerings that answer those needs, solve the customer's problems, and relieve pains.

High-return businesses realize that their salespeople can also gather information about the types of offerings that should be developed in the future. The salesperson's customer discussions are at once part of the execution of today's strategy, and key elements in the planning of the firm's future strategies. The salespersons' discussion is key to successful strategy and execution.

Harley-Davidson's salespeople were so mentally intertwined with their customers that one could not tell them apart, literally. In the 1980s and 1990s, the firm showed a rise in return on investment that was phenomenal. A healthy customer-directed selling process is important for selling more motorcycles today and for planning the types of bikes to build tomorrow.

A strategy-and-execution continuum in manufacturing

During periods of great performance at firms, the shop floor personnel who are manufacturing the products for today are also contributing ideas and insights for more effectively creating and delivering the products of tomorrow.

The kaizen system in Japan is a model of continuous improvement in the manufacturing process, achieving more effective and efficient production of goods. The term, kaizen, means continuous improvement. Toyota Motor Company's encouragement of the participation from the shop floor has been essential to its high quality vehicle production, an offering that for years could be matched by few at similar price points.

Every time a task is performed, there is some result that should feed back into reconsidering and restructuring of the plan, on an ongoing basis. This concept holds for every area of high-return organizations. The implementation of existing plans today is part and parcel of the strategizing of the plans for tomorrow.

Need to plan *executability*

"Our strategy was sound, but we failed in execution."

Planning and execution should not be considered as distinctly separate concepts. Doing so causes one to miss the importance of the continuum of strategy and execution.

Toys R Us has experienced a decline in cash flow returns for almost 20 years straight. Once the leader in toy sales, it has fallen behind dramatically. The firm has attempted to create new plans and strategies, but some of these are glaring examples of a failure to fill in the gaps between planning and implementation.

In the late 1990s, when the toy company realized that the Internet and the World Wide Web would be a dominant force in retail, it began to plan an online presence, www.toysrus.com. The strategy seemed to make sense.

Competitive analysis would have shown that Toys R Us had a powerful brand that would be strongly recognized online as it was offline. Unlike other online toy retailers, like the now defunct eToys, Toys R US had warehouses chock full of inventory, ready to be sold. Its purchasing capability for restocking its shelves was strong. All necessary toy manufacturer relationships had already been established, something a new online toy company simply couldn't replicate in short order.

However, the firm failed to *plan executability,* a concept that occupies the space between planning and implementation.

Toysrus.com succeeded in generating very high online sales. The site attracted millions of visitors who purchased toys online well-before the Christmas holiday that year. It was also a complete disaster.

The company failed to determine whether or not the toy warehouses were capable of "pick-and-pack" shipping methods. Instead, the inventory management system in place at Toys R Us warehouses was designed to ship entire pallets of toys at a time to be stocked at the store shelves. Loading a crate of 100 Barbie Dolls onto a truck is entirely different from physically picking up just one Barbie and packaging it in a box with three or four other individually picked toys.

The firm disappointed customers in the thousands, failing to deliver promised toys by Christmas time, and forcing untold levels of havoc at the physical stores where people went to express their online-generated grievances. Many customers swore they would never buy from Toys R Us again, online or physically at a store.

Of pilots and parallels

Could this toysrus.com failure be attributed to poor strategy or poor execution? Any answer would require an arbitrary definition of the two concepts. Many of the problems that TOY experienced in execution could have been discovered if *executability* had been given appropriate attention in strategic planning phases. The important point is that in the continuum of planning and implementation there should be *planning of implementation.*

Every high-return business knows that it should never install a new computer system without running it first in parallel with the existing systems.

Firms are famous for having 'beta' launches in place for years before the 'official' release of the product. Every great product launch includes pilot launches, test cases, use cases, dress rehearsals, and other means of making sure that the execution of a particular strategy is plausible and reasonable, before widespread implementation of the plan.

At what level of shipping activity might a plant floor manager at Toys R Us have realized that, *"Our warehouses are just not set up for this kind of pick-and-pack inventory management?"* Ideally, at some earlier stage than when it was already too late.

If a manager had to choose, angering a small set of test customers is far better than angering a large group of them. Planning executability is a necessary part of strategic planning, with the three higher tenets as the primary goals of that planning process.

When the execution may not matter

During the 9/11 terrorist attacks on the United States, what was the only mobile system that appeared to work without fail? The Iridium satellite phone system by Motorola.

Iridium was also the mobile phone system that worked most flawlessly during the Northeast USA electricity blackout in 2003. The system has worked on oil rigs in the middle of the oceans. It has also worked in deserts, in arctic expeditions, and in a number of places and during periods of time where no other phone communication has been possible. In the category of 'operational effectiveness,' Iridium is a marvel of technology. The business has also lost billions of dollars.

The failure of Iridium as a business unit at Motorola cannot be attributed to plan implementation, given the system's operational effectiveness. The issue was in the original strategy. A firm cannot afford to expend countless dollars of investments and years of human resources on an initiative with questionable ability to achieve the Goal Tenets of strategy. There simply weren't enough customers who were able to pay high enough prices to justify the amount of resources that Iridium absorbed to deliver its offering, no matter how effective the units.

While the development of the offering was sound, the estimate of the level of need for the offering was not sound. Iridium at Motorola was a perfect example of great execution of an inadequate strategy. Motorola sold off the business after great losses.

The right execution tool for the right strategic job

Every year, a new crop of 'branded' implementation methodologies appears. Each of these methods focuses on some aspect of producing offerings more effectively and efficiently. More popular ones include Six Sigma, Balanced Scorecard, TQM for Total Quality Management, and Lean Manufacturing. There are far too many to mention them all, but these are certainly ones worth noting.

One of the founding fathers of these systems was the late W. Edwards Deming. Probably no foreigner has ever had so positive an impact on Japan's manufacturing prowess and success as he. Deming focused management teams on quality of product and quality controls. Improvement came by identifying sources of business dysfunction of many kinds. Deming's system was termed TQM for Total Quality Management and is the foundation of many other programs.

Six Sigma has its roots in Deming's research and teachings back to the 1940s and 1950s. The Six Sigma program has been widely cited alongside the high returns generated at General Electric. Black Belts of the Six Sigma program, as they are called, focus on statistical controls and the famous goal of 'less than 3.4 defects per one million products.' Companies using this program seek this level of quality control in their production.

Meanwhile, lean manufacturers focus on reducing the resources required to produce a given number of goods, freeing up society's resources while attempting to accomplish higher levels of production and efficiency goals.

Balanced Scorecards are another popular system for ensuring that strategies are executed as planned. Similar concepts are known as Value-Based Management, Dashboards, and others. Based on a review of company annual reports (10Ks), well over half of the 500 largest companies in the US have implemented this system in one shape or another. They focus on this adage:

"If you can't measure it, you can't manage it."

Balanced Scorecard initiatives highlight the importance of balancing measures and metrics in the business, including financial, customer, internal process, and growth and innovation perspectives of an organization. Another important concept is the understanding of the lagging and leading nature of various indicators.

Making sense of it all

Experienced operations consultants describe a funny story about the various ways operational improvement could be focused.

> *Do you know the difference between the optimist and the pessimist? Or, the difference between the lean manufacturer and the six sigma practitioner?*
>
> *The optimist sees the glass as half-full. The pessimist sees the glass as half-empty.*
>
> *The lean manufacturer will quickly point out the inefficiencies in the glass being too big, instructing for reduction in the size of the glass.*
>
> *The expert in Six-Sigma will say, "Who cares about the glass? Tell me about the quality of the water inside it."*

Of course, the truly enlightened will ask whether or not anyone will buy this particular glass of water, and at how high a price-point.

Management can be confused as to what type of 'execution program' is appropriate for the business at hand. Every day, another company touts its use of one of these programs, often cited as the panacea toward improved cash flows. Yet, by and large, there is no correlation between high cash flow returns and the implementation of any specific program. Firms may generate *higher* returns than they would have otherwise, but those returns may still remain below the cost of capital.

The Balanced Scorecard is one of the most popular strategy execution frameworks in use today. Many companies have achieved improvements in performance using this approach and others have failed to do so. Six Sigma appears to be used regularly at firms with mediocre returns. Sophisticated methods for operational effectiveness, no matter how well-named, are not enough to drive good returns if the firm fails at achieving the higher tenets.

Why not just combine all these operations programs?

Some retailers such as Wal-Mart and Target have shown inconsistent pricing of their products. Frequently, the same basket of goods purchased at one of these retailers varies from the same basket purchased the same day at another store, or at the same store on different days, *often different than advertised price*. If done with unethical purposes, such as a bait-and-switch technique, this flaw could generate the ire of regulatory authorities.

However, if sometimes materially inaccurate pricing is a natural state of an operation that seeks the lowest overall prices, maybe customers simply don't care. In other words, would customers desire a business to provide 100% accurate pricing, if that required the business to implement systems that increased the prices overall? Doubtful. Retail customers seem to not to be overly concerned with perfectly accurate pricing per product so long as they achieve lower costs prices overall – and that the errors seem to go both ways, not always in the retailer's favor.

Execution that's right for one strategy, wrong for another

The explicit 'defects per million' target implicit in the name 'Six Sigma' may be overkill for some activities and yet far too lenient for others. In airline safety, is Six Sigma a reasonable target of flawlessness? Of course not. Given 10 million domestic flights in the United States in a year, would consumers be satisfied with 'only' 34 plane crashes per year? Something far more stringent is necessary, and demands the effort required.

The right execution at the right stage

During the 1980s and 1990s, pharmaceutical and medical device firms such as Abbott, Pfizer, and Medtronic exhibited some of the most consistently high returns, year after year. At early stages of the drug and device development pipeline, one would expect to have many, many failures. Successful research, discovery, and the process of creativity require lots of failed attempts and trials.

Meanwhile, at the end of the pipeline when drugs and devices are provided directly to patients, defects need to be zero as people's lives may be on the line. The right systems, processes, and entire way of thinking at the beginning of the process should be dramatically different from that at the other end. High return firms recognize this and act accordingly. As Deming has said, when choosing the right focus for implementation,

> *"Don't adopt... adapt."*

High-performance firms fit the right methods for execution given the strategy in place. They don't simply implement 'Six Sigma' because of GE's reputation and use of it, regardless of how high GE's returns may be.

In delivering what's promised, failure is not an option

Customers express deep anger toward firms that do not provide what's promised. Business success is dependent on effectively delivering the offerings that the firm has branded in the minds of its customers. The difficulty is in understanding exactly what the customer expects, and not over-delivering on things they don't determine as valuable.

Every execution plan must include a compensation plan

People do what they are paid to do. No matter what plan for executability is in place, compensation programs need to be aligned with it. Short-term and long-term strategies require short-term and long-term forms of compensation. Any form of compensation of employees, whether monetary or otherwise, needs to be aligned with the strategies in place. Without a well-aligned compensation plan, one can be sure that any plan for execution is suspect.

Tenet Four is number four for a reason

In the early 1980s, the Ford Company hired Deming and was able to successfully improve its execution and thereby the quality of vehicles. Donald E. Petersen, then Chairman of the Board of Ford Motor Company, said the following:

> *"I'm proud to say I'm a Deming disciple, and we at Ford are committed to his operating principles, particularly to the ethic of continuous improvement and the involvement of all employees."*

Despite this, over the long term, larger issues loomed for the company – in terms of target markets, needs identification, and other aspects of the business strategy. Adopting a quality-based mentality is commendable, but insufficient to long-term high-return generation and business success.

Concluding notes on Tenet Four

The focus of Tenet Four must be squarely on achieving Tenets One, Two, and Three. High return businesses bypass unnecessary conceptual debates that artificially separate strategy and execution. Cash flow returns follow a focus on the executability of plans and the effective and efficient delivery of planned offerings.

Shall we build the operations necessary for highest quality or lowest cost? There is little potential for achieving both. Should management seek an inventory system devoid of stock-outs with always available product, or the absolute leanest inventories and assets in a system that requires more lead time?

The answer to these questions comes from executing on plans as identified by focusing on the higher tenets.

As the strategies of today are executed, the results must drive a reconsideration of those strategies, as soon as the results would imply. In many respects, the implementation of plans today is simultaneously part of the plan development of tomorrow. Strategy and execution are different focal points of a great business process.

The central placement of Tenet Four in the Return Driven Strategy pyramid – and the word 'driven' in Return Driven Strategy – suggest that execution is the heart of any great business strategy. Which is more important, strategy or execution? Both.

Key Diagnostics for Tenet Four

Does management have a strategy for execution aimed at realistically being able to deliver offerings to the degree planned, designed, and promised, that align with the customer-oriented Tenets Two and Three?

Does management have an ongoing process for revisiting strategy in line with the information received through other aspects of business operations?

Does the business perform its operations – from back-offices to production to marketing to sales and to delivery – in ways consistent with Tenets Two and Three, and never in violation of Tenet One?

Does the business use Genuine Assets to better assure achievement of this tenet? Is a process in place for building these Genuine Assets?

Is management continually on the watch for and aware of significant forces of change that could limit the firm's ability to execute on Tenet Four in the future?

Are the right metrics in place and reviewed regularly to help management monitor and communicate the business's ability to execute on Tenet Four?

General Electric (GE)

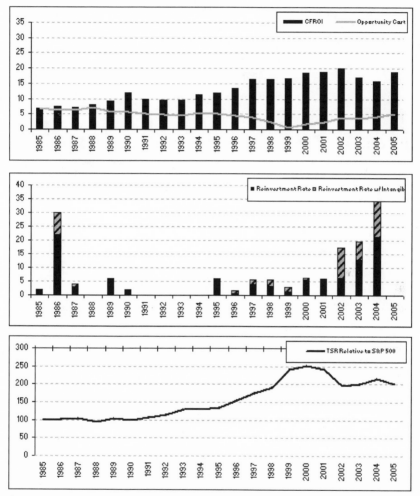

GE is renowned world-wide for its ability to operate effectively and efficiently. With programs like Six Sigma, the firm displays consistently high CFROI levels. This feat is all the more compelling when viewed in light of the massive asset base upon which GE generates its returns.

Increasing CFROI returns on investment are reflected in an impressive stock price rise from 1985 through 2001. After 2001, CFROI levels remain high, but not increasingly higher and the sheer enormity of the firm makes high growth rates near impossible except by acquisition. Valuations then stagnate.

Ford (F)

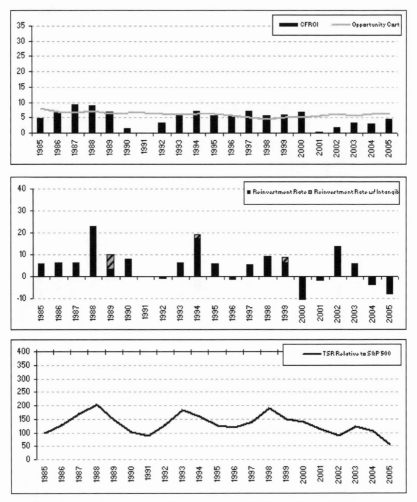

- The influx of Deming's Total Quality Management initiatives years ago may have been a driver of vehicle quality improvement at Ford that many now say is on par with the highly-regarded European automakers. However, functional quality is not enough to generate high returns. If Tenet Four is not properly aligned with proper targeting of otherwise unmet customer needs, quality products may be made, but simply not sold to enough customers, or at prices not high enough.

The low CFROI returns and cyclical growth rates combine to form a rocky valuation pattern over 20 years, unfortunately with a downward trend.

Toyota (7203)

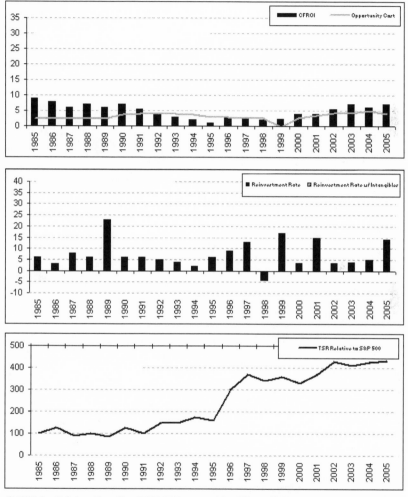

Toyota is credited with building operational systems that have created vehicles with a reputation for low-maintenance and higher lasting value. For such a
large industry this strategy can take years and years to develop.

In the mid 1990s, Toyota's returns show a firm that seems to be more focused on sales and growth than on profitability. However, as the firm's business
shifts into higher CFROI levels from 2000 to 2005, the positive returns on the
massive asset base begin to produce giant jumps in stock price.

Motorola (MOT)

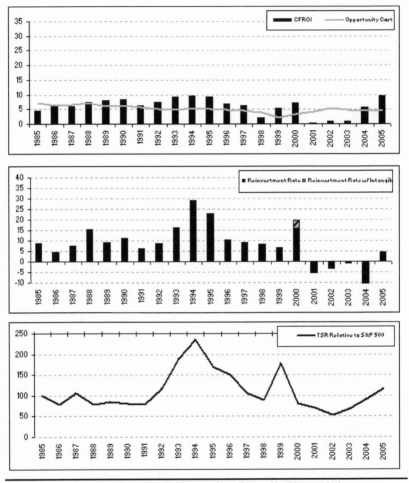

Motorola is known for having built methods for superior operations and execution. The firm is credited with building the original Six Sigma frameworks for which GE is known. Motorola was also known for its use of the Balanced Scorecard in ensuring execution of stated objectives.

Unfortunately, as the CFROI levels show in the top panel, effective delivery of offerings is not enough, if delivered to the wrong customers or targeting the wrong needs. The firm's rocky stock price and cyclical return and growth profile represent issues that are beyond operational excellence, namely with the higher Tenets Two and Three.

DRIVEN

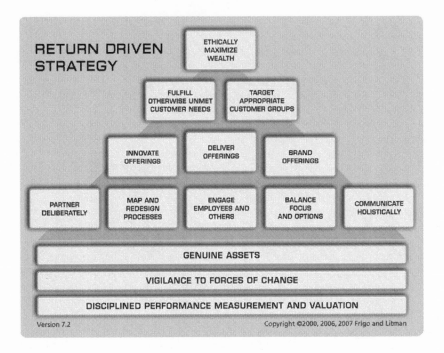

Tenet Five

Innovate Offerings

Tenet Five is the second of the three 'Competency Tenets' of a Return-Driven organization. Through the innovation of offerings, more and more needs can be met, and businesses succeed.

- Inspire the innovation of offerings by continually gaining detailed, insightful information about customers' primary unmet needs

- Innovate the entirety of the offering, focusing not only on its function, but also on all of the psychological attributes and influences an offering could potentially deliver for the fulfillment of need

- Beware of innovation for innovation's sake, and ensure that customer needs are always the focus of innovation

- Separate between innovation of offerings and innovation of processes. Process innovation is important to offering delivery and other tenets, but process innovation is insufficient in innovating for new offering development.

- Recognize the importance of failure in innovation; failure at the right time and at the right levels is absolutely necessary for successful innovation toward the achievement of extraordinary performance

- Employ Genuine Assets that allow the firm to innovate in ways that other firms cannot.

- Be vigilant to forces of change that continually impact the types of offerings that should be innovated, as well as the means for innovating them

- Create and manage for the measures that encourage innovation, allowing for failures and mistakes, and always with a focus of the creation and delivery of offerings to achieve the higher tenets

Inspiration for innovation

Inspiration, invention, and ingenuity all describe ways in which creativity is channeled toward developing offerings that fulfill the needs of targeted customer groups. High return businesses harness creative endeavors not simply for improving products and services, but for dreaming up, developing, and delivering any possible offering that fulfills needs in ways no other offering previously has.

In the third level of the Return Driven Strategy pyramid, innovation of offerings is one of the necessary competencies for any successful business. Firms with the highest returns have skills, experience, and a focused intention for changing their offerings on an ongoing basis.

Medtronic's impressive financial performance is driven by its focus on its mission statement, in place since the 1960s:

> *"To contribute to human welfare by application of biomedical engineering in the research, design, manufacture, and sale of instruments or appliances that alleviate pain, restore health, and extend life."*

The firm's focus is a great example of how innovation, offerings, and needs are defined together as the path to the creation of wealth. In one statement, Medtronic reflects most of the top of the Return Driven Strategy pyramid.

Innovation stems from creativity and experimentation. This process is not limited to firms in so-called creative industries like advertising, design, or scientific fields. Regardless of industry, with no exceptions, innovation has been a core element of every firm that has ever sustained high returns and growth rates for any notable duration of time.

Not innovation for innovation's sake

It's not enough that a firm be creative. The intention behind innovation needs to be focused on the creation of new offerings that answer needs that customers cannot get answered elsewhere. Innovation activities are not necessarily represented by expenditures of research and development.

Any change in activity is a behavior that can potentially represent innovation in the most general sense of the term. For this reason, identifying activities directed toward innovation *of offerings* can be difficult.

Research and development expenditures are a crude measure for innovation. However, based on research using HOLT's extensive cash flow database, companies that report large research and development (R&D greater than 10% of capital invested or sales) tend to have higher relative valuation levels than firms that don't report any R&D expense, on average, over time.

Obviously, one should not conclude that by simply spending more incrementally on R&D that a firm's valuation will improve. It all depends on how that R&D is being spent.

Not innovation for the sake of internal processes

When considering the process of innovation at his firm, one manager asked, *"Should we be technology-driven or market-driven?"* It's an interesting question of a type that comes up regularly.

Another manager stated a specific need for innovation in a specific instance. *"We have manufacturing capacity. We're innovating new products to use up that capacity."*

General uses of the term, 'innovation,' may be important to a company, such as innovating systems and internal processes. Being cognizant of necessary changes in the business is key to every tenet. Improvement of a manufacturing process that reduces costs could be seen as an 'innovation,' but it's not the focus of this tenet. Innovation of processes is important, but in this example it's part of Tenet Four, executability and ensuring efficient offering delivery.

Many technology companies have an existing platform to build on. This could be an important asset to the firm, but it could also be a distraction against longer-term success. 'Assets' are worthless to a business if they don't lead to future cash flows.

What's the answer to the question, *"Should we be technology-driven or market-driven?"* Offering innovation should be *return driven,* regardless of existing technology platforms or historical lines of business. That means targeting otherwise unmet customer needs for large enough customer groups to justify the resources required for innovation.

Innovating the entirety of the offering

There are always opportunities for new offerings that answer existing unmet needs. Return-driven firms consider all aspects of a potential or existing offering and 'what it does' for the customer. This may include a traditional product component, a service component, or a psychological component. Businesses, particularly salespeople, will often talk about focusing less on the features of an offering and more on the benefits to the customer. This is on the right track, but can be taken a step farther. The focus should be squarely on otherwise unmet customer needs.

Therefore, successful businesses innovate anything that affects the customer's mental perception of an offering. How the customer receives the offering can be as important as the physical functions of the offering. For Dell in the late 1980s and 1990s, the singular experience of the direct model, allowing customers a myriad of self-selected choices in building their personal computer, was as important to the offering as the computer itself. At the time, it fulfilled an unmet need, but one that is now equally well met by a number of direct-model computer companies.

Innovation when previous offerings are dying

Some businesses are faced with the problem of having offerings that target needs that no longer exist. Companies that produced buggy-whips just before the advent of motor cars were naturally marked by falling sales volumes and falling prices. The failure of companies like Polaroid and Kodak to move quickly into digital photography, despite the assets available to them, was a contributor to poor performance.

The solution is a release of the attachment to existing product and service lines. Firm's that have continually generated high returns have noticed how their Genuine Assets could be leveraged in new ways toward new offerings for new target needs. GE makes more than refrigerators. Wal-Mart is far more than a department store. Toyota makes luxury Lexus vehicles. Nokia is no longer a paper company, but a manufacturer of telecom equipment.

Innovation for offerings with no pricing power

In commoditized industries, pricing competition rules the day. Sales volumes may hold, but pricing per unit falters. With perfect substitutes available, customers force firms to compete on price. Essentially, the businesses are able to sell offerings that do fulfill needs, just not *otherwise unmet* ones.

Innovation is the only viable solution to the commoditization of goods. It can even save an entire industry. While pricing is tough, the fact that sales volumes remain stable implies there is a ray of hope.

Every business that has displayed high performance over long-terms has shown an ability 'to reinvent itself' as if the business were dying. Some successful firms have chosen to move into entirely new industries, while others simply step-out into related industries.

The paper industry is a perfect example of these issues. General paper manufacturing has been a case study in a commoditized industry. Despite the advent of the digital age, society remains dependent on paper. We are surrounded by it. With no differentiation and perfect substitutes available, it's impossible for paper firms to sustain decent profits.

Nokia's strategic move from paper-manufacturing to mobile phones was a dramatic one that took years to bring about, but with incredible success. Meanwhile, Kimberly-Clark has shown more steady change in business focus from paper-manufacturing to branded paper products like Kleenex and now beyond that into all kinds of consumer products.

Innovation means experimentation

High-performance firms fail 'small and often' in order to succeed big. The road to returns is paved with failure as a regular part of every day. It's impossible to innovate without making mistakes. The key to innovation is making mistakes at the right levels and at the right times. Business plans, compensation plans, and cultures need to reflect this.

Management teams will create compensation plans that do not allow for failure, with fixed targets and fixed payments.

This doesn't mean that business should pay for failure. It simply suggests that as failures are necessary to success, compensation plans and all plans for execution must address the issue ahead of time.

Failure IS an option in offering development

"We pay for results. We can't afford mistakes."

For some business activities, this statement reflects the attitude required for proper execution. However, this kind of thinking can kill future returns if it pervades the culture of the entire firm. Small failures are necessary to innovation, at the right places and at the right stages.

In the early 1990s, Wal-Mart invested heavily in Sam's Clubs, but pulled back as they didn't provide returns the way the Wal-Mart stores did. Home Depot had a similar experience with its EXPO line. Coca-Cola changed the formula from its flagship Coca-Cola product to New Coke, only to change it back later. In each of these cases, the firms may have expended more on the mistakes than they should have, but overall company returns remained strong nonetheless. It takes a management team with big shoulders to take big risks, and even bigger shoulders to admit mistakes.

As in life, admitting failures and moving forward are natural aspects of successful management teams. Bill Gates admitted that one of his biggest mistakes was missing the importance of the Internet protocol (TCP/IP) in the future of technology. With some of the highest returns over decades, Microsoft recovered. In contrast, firms that 'fail big' are ones that often refuse to admit failure in the first place.

One business strategy myth is the belief that firms need to make big bets in order to succeed. The extensive research of corporate cash flows shows strong evidence that 'big bet' strategies are not how firms succeed over the long haul.

One notable example is represented by Charles Schwab's first forays into a number of separate electronic trading platforms such as StreetSmart and eSchwab before it centered on the Schwab.com organization as people know it today, one totally integrated with the bricks-and-mortar side of the business. The smaller business trials created a foundation of learning that eventually drove Schwab to become an incredibly high return business.

Concluding notes on Tenet Five

Inspiration and innovation are real sources of wealth-creation. With customers who perceive unlimited needs, unlimited opportunities are available. Trouble exists mostly when firms focus all efforts on existing offerings instead of continually looking for new ways of fulfilling needs.

Innovation is placed as Tenet Five not because it is fifth in importance, but because innovation must follow intention. When creativity is channeled through the intention of the higher tenets, more of the ills of society can be solved. As creative as an organization can be, it must still deliver an offering that fulfills the unmet needs of large enough customer groups to support the resources for the creativity.

Return-driven firms balance some business activities on exploration and other activities on delivery. The balance between these two is determined by forecasting and measuring the firm's results.

Key Diagnostics for Tenet Five

Is the business's innovation focused squarely on customers' otherwise unmet needs as defined by Tenets Two and Three?

Is there a specific concept and initiative for the innovating of offerings (and not simply the innovation of processes)?

Does innovation focus on the entirety of the offering, including the psychological value, the derivative value, and the entire sales chain – and not simply functional attributes?

When moving from research to actual offering development, is the executability of delivering the new offering being taken into consideration?

Are all innovation activities performed within the ethical parameters of the business's communities? Are investments in innovation made consistently within a focus on maximizing wealth-creation?

Does the business use Genuine Assets to better assure achievement of this tenet? Is a process is in place for building these Genuine Assets?

Is management continually on the watch for and aware of significant forces of change that could limit the firm's ability to execute on Tenet Five in the future?

Are the right metrics in place and reviewed regularly to help management monitor and communicate the business's ability to execute on Tenet Five?

Medtronic (MDT)

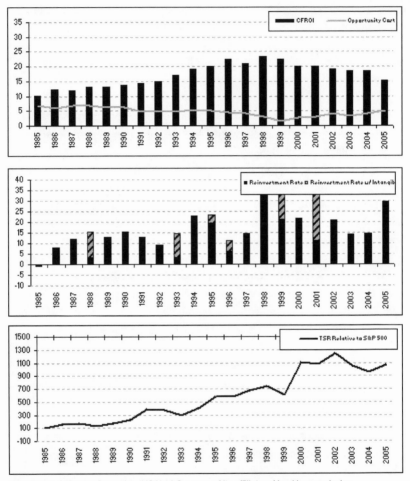

High CFROI return levels and high growth rates have driven Medtronic's valuation to stock price performance more than 10 times the US market average. The company motto states its purpose and path to wealth-creation: *Alleviating Pain, Restoring Health, Extending Life.* This succinct, well-defined, and targeted customer need creates a platform for unlimited offering innovation, and thereby wealth-creation.

Medtronic's history is suited for explaining any tenet in the entire Return Driven Strategy framework, in particular, *Innovate Offerings.*

Intel Corp (INTC)

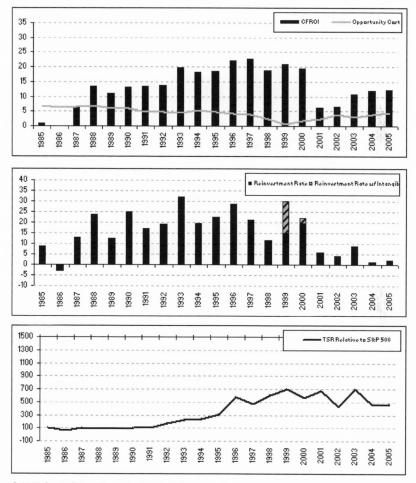

The importance of innovation is well-implied by this famous quote by the co-founder of Intel, Gordon Moore, namely, Moore's Law. It states that the power of a computer chip *doubles every two years.*

Intel has shown an ability to remain at the forefront of innovating the computer chip, contributing both to an increase in the power of computers and decrease in the cost of them. A stock price rising more than five times the US market average has been driven by high CFROI returns and growth rates through the year 2000. Since then, markets appear to be saturated, yielding lower growth rates, but ongoing innovation works to keep CFROI levels above the cost of capital.

111

Schering-Plough (SGP)

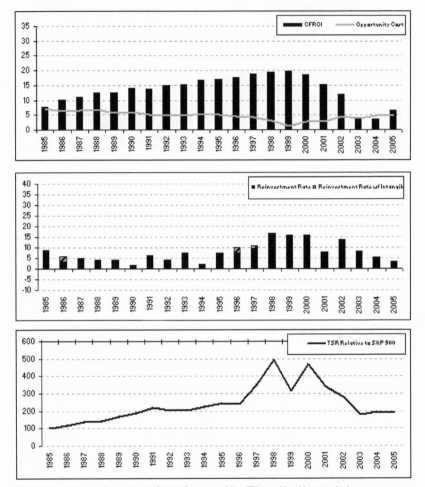

In the pharmaceutical industry, the life cycle of a drug from earliest inception to customer purchase can be more than ten years. For this reason, investments in the innovation of offerings, research, and development, are properly reflected in the asset growth/reinvestment rate of the firm.

Schering-Plough's low reinvestment rates in the late 1980s and early 1990s may have been a key cause of the failure to innovate new offerings years later. Old profitable drugs were not being sufficiently replaced by new ones from 2000 to 2003, as plummeting CFROI levels and stock price show.

Nokia (NOK1V)

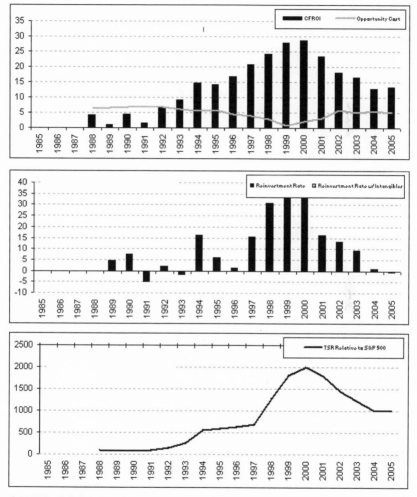

Once a paper company, now a telecom giant. In its move away from low CFROI level, commoditized businesses, the Finland-based Nokia focused on mobile phones and telecom equipment. The high growth rates from ongoing innovations have made it the largest mobile phone manufacturer in the world.

High CFROI returns and compounding growth rates drove the phenomenal stock price rise through 2000. Since then, market saturation of phones and increasing availability of substitute offerings have led to a collapse in growth. The relatively high CFROI levels have kept the stock from losing all of its previously-set gains.

113

eBay (EBAY)

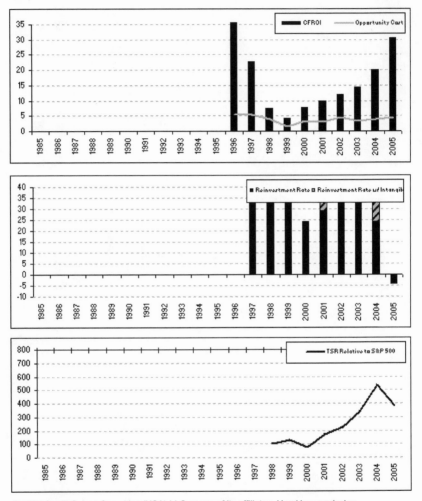

By targeting the need for liquidity and efficiency in the auction and sale of goods, eBay's meteoric rise has been unabated. The value of the eBay community increases exponentially from the network effect of having more members. This creates a natural monopoly that is very difficult to break, as the monopoly occurs through the voluntary acts of buyers and sellers going where everyone else already happens to be. Over the time period shown above, eBay continually innovated its offerings, opening more types of auctions and other related services.

Separately, as all three panels of year 2005 show, despite a high CFROI level, higher valuations require growth in capital investment as well. As growth fell, so did valuation, incrementally.

DRIVEN

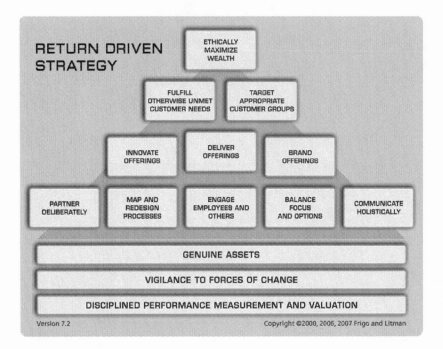

Tenet Six

Brand Offerings

Tenet Six is third of the three 'Competency Tenets' of a Return-Driven organization. 'Brand' is a verb that describes what the firm should do to the offering. Branding is a core component of any high-performance firm, when focused on achievement of the higher tenets, and when the *purpose* of branding is not confused with the *tools*.

- View brands as psychological bridges that can create an indelible connection in the mind of the customer between the firm's offering and the need it fulfills

- Brand consistently with the delivery of the offering in order to create the strongest mental connection; high return firms do not attempt to brand offerings around promises that the customer perceives cannot be delivered

- Separate the concepts of branding and advertising; advertising is a communication tool for branding and other firm goals, but should not be confused with the purpose

- Employ Genuine Assets that allow the firm to make the strongest bridge possible when branding

- Be vigilant to forces of change that continually affect each sides of the branding bridge, the offering and the needs, and the ability and means for making that connection

- Build and manage branding measures that always lead to achievement of the higher tenets; branding recognition and awareness metrics are troublesome if they cannot link to customer purchase and pricing

In the creation of wealth, brands are bridges

To create wealth, proper branding activities build an indelible connection in the mind of the customer between the customer's explicitly understood need and the offering that uniquely fulfills it. A successful bridge with strong foundations on both sides of the bridge – the offering and the need – results in an exchange between the firm and the customer.

Successful branding doesn't occur in television commercials. It doesn't occur in print ads, billboards, product labels or any other place, save one. The branding process is psychological, and can only occur in the mind of the customer. Everything else is a tool for branding and so anything that impacts the customer's mind about the offering is branding the offering

Brand the offering AND the need at the same time

Assuming an offering can be delivered that fulfills otherwise unmet need, branding activities should brand the need as well as the offering. For whatever reason, this seems not to be so obvious. It's not enough that a customer have an unmet need. The customer must also be *explicitly aware of it.* No matter how much the business knows that the need exists, the customer isn't going to buy without being self-aware of that need. There must be terra firma, so to speak, on both sides of the bridge. *Need awareness* is as important as *brand awareness.*

Branding does not create the need

The psychological nature of the branding process can create misconceptions about what exactly is happening.

> *"Our advertising campaign successfully created the need for our product."*

Branding cannot create a human need. However, when done success-fully, it can help the customer to identify and become aware of it. It may appear that need has been created, but upon deeper analysis, one finds the need was always there. The branding activities merely fo-cused the customer's attention on it.

The invention and development of the Internet has led to products and services that never before existed. These include email, chat rooms, blogs, online auctions, and others. Certainly, there has been quite a lot of advertising and branding to promote the use of email and the Inter-net in general, and adoption has been incredible.

Yet, did the branding create the need for these new services, where a need for them never before existed? On the contrary, the new services simply created new offerings targeted at previously existing needs. Email, chat rooms, and blogs are just a few of the ways that customers achieve a sense of community, connectedness to others, and more communication with others. These are basic human needs.

The branding and marketing efforts elicited the awareness of the need and how the new offerings could fulfill them. The need for email did not need to be created. The need for blogs did not require develop-ment. The need was always there in the first place. The offerings were simply new tools for fulfilling it.

Brand the offering and need, not the company

Many times, firms spend millions on branding the company name. Sometimes managers will believe customers' awareness of the name of the business will lead to sales of the business's offerings. Some publicly traded companies even believed that awareness of the com-pany name can benefit the stock price.

> *"After all, if more potential investors knew about our firm, maybe they'd be more likely to purchase our stock."*

In reality, this may lead to short term fluctuations, but valuation levels achieved this way are unsustainable. This thinking stems from a lack of understanding of what really drives stock price levels.

Webvan was a company that sought to leverage the Internet to allow customers to purchase groceries online which would then be delivered to their homes. There are companies that have found enough customers and business partners to make this a viable business. However, it wasn't viable for Webvan, and the firm went bankrupt. Among other things, frivolous spending in advertising hurt the business.

Webvan was spending advertising dollars with one of the top Internet portal and search engine firms. Visitors to the portal would see advertising that Webvan had purchased. The company advertised nationally through the US, but most of the US couldn't use their offering. The firm was only in a handful of the top US cities, yet almost anyone in the US who visited the portal would see the firm's online ads.

At this time, however, the search engine firm already had the ability to focus its advertisers' communications toward people in the geographic areas where the Webvan service was available, and offered that selective advertising to Webvan. The firm turned them down, and specifically chose to advertise nationwide anyway. Why would a firm advertise to every person in the US and abroad, when only a small fraction could actually use the service?

One belief was that the firm saw the advertising as communicating the firm's stock to prospective individual investors. This represents a misunderstanding of stock prices. If a particular company stock is viable and undervalued, there are more than enough investors to know about it. In fact, there are more money managers in the United States examining and purchasing stocks *than there are stocks*.

There are cases of tiny or new companies that need to make them known among likely investors. However, there are many methods of investor relations far more effective and economical than advertising nationwide in portals.

Pharmaceutical companies spend billions in advertising and promotions in order to brand their products. Many of them have enjoyed some of the most consistently high returns for decades. Throughout the 1980s and 1990s, Abbott, Johnson & Johnson, and Pfizer grew to be multi-billion-dollar revenue giants. How many would know that the popular nutritional bars found in groceries called ZonePerfect were products of Abbott? Few might know that the popular Listerine mouthwash was once a product of Pfizer, or that Rolaids is a product of Johnson & Johnson.

If the goal of the firm is revenues and profitability, brand the offering and the need, not the name of the business, unless that company name is part of the offering communication, as in umbrella branding.

Umbrella branding

The Marriott Hotel brand sits behind the Fairfield Inn, Courtyards, Residence Inn, and other brands. In this case, that umbrella brand communicates something about the hotels that while each is different, they share traits in terms of level of cleanliness, reservation terms, frequent stay programs, or other attributes. The purpose of advertising Marriott alongside its individual brands is that it communicates something to the customer about the offering.

Advertising is a tool, but only one of many

The mission of branding is often confused with the tool of advertising. Branding is not advertising. Advertising is a tool to brand, but should never be confused with the process of branding itself.

In their book, *The 22 Immutable Laws of Branding,* Al and Laura Ries discuss the over-dependence on advertising when many firms seek to build a brand. They contend that great brands are built not through advertising but through public relations. Advertising is simply a tool to keep the brand healthy. The research of the Ries father-and-daughter team is entirely consistent with Return Driven Strategy.

In the early 2000s when the recruiting company Monster.com was ramping up its operations, the company purchased the most expensive advertising spots during the Super Bowl. The company received extremely high levels of press by being the number one spender. The public relations Monster received after the Super Bowl far outweighed the reach from the Super Bowl ads them. That level of spending generated almost unbelievable public relations (PR) activity. Almost no one would remember the second highest spender for that Super Bowl.

The value of Monster.com's spending was in the PR more than in the advert itself.

Advertising can create brand awareness and brand recognition. However, these objectives can distract from the real goal of branding which is to convince customers that their unmet needs can be uniquely fulfilled with the offering. Awareness or recognition of a brand is useless if the customer does not buy. In the end, if the person doesn't purchase, then all the activities that attempt to cause that branding to happen are a waste of resources. Without purchase, branding efforts cannot be considered worthwhile.

What influences branding

Every customer touch-point is a branding opportunity, where the customer's mind can be influenced. Branding occurs through the customer's thoughts and feelings regarding the offering and the need. It occurs whether the business initiates that influence or not. The ideas surrounding a particular offering are heavily affected by the customer's ongoing interactions with anything that affects that bridge.

Branding activities encompass absolutely anything that can impact the two sides of the branding process: the offering and the need in the mind of the customer. Certainly, advertising can be one way of doing this, but so are many other forms of communications:

> Public relations
> Face-to-face sales meetings or even door-to-door
> Coupons and promotions
> Point-of-sale communications
> Point of usage communications
> Billing and invoicing

Can the brand do it all?

The popular press is replete with information about the value of 'brands,' often even citing specific dollar values to the company of the brand itself versus the rest of the company's market or book value. The valuation methodologies behind these lists are suspect at best.

Seldom is there adequate evidence tying the valuation back to the underlying cash flows of the firm.

The problem is that the value of the brand cannot be separated from the cash flows of the offering with which it is associated. Even if a company were to purchase the licensing of a specific name, without an offering to attach the name to, and a need that the offering fulfills, the brand remains worthless.

Branding shows up number six in the Eleven Tenets for a reason. Coca-Cola has been cited for decades as one of the world's top brands. However, it was during the 1980s and 1990s that the firm really began to generate remarkable cash flow returns. From 1985 to 1997, returns accelerated from 14% to 40%. Was the Coca-Cola brand so different in the minds of the consumers from the beginning of that period until the end? Or, was something else responsible for the firm's incredible returns and associated stock price rise?

As the man who ran Coca-cola during that time-frame stated, far more than a brand is necessary to create a great business. Roberto Goizueta, for whom an entire MBA program is named, spoke of the value of branding and advertising quite bluntly:

> *"You let me have the bottling plants and*
> *the trucks and the highly efficient systems,*
> *and I'll let you have the TV commercials.*
> *I'll beat you to a pulp over time."*

From "How Coke is Kicking Pepsi's Can." Fortune Oct 1996

What's the value today of the brands of Polaroid and its instant photographs or Betamax and its video tape format? Many consumers still remember these names vividly. Yet, without the innovation of a deliverable offering that fulfills unmet needs, brands are worth significantly less, if anything at all.

The other extreme: If you build it, will they come?

Customers have scarce resources, not just of money, but of time. There is real value to the customer for initiatives that help them to make quicker decisions about a particular offering simply by being aware of the reputation associated with the brand.

One of the first top mobile communications companies was a firm called Glenayre Technologies. Today, few know the company name or its products. The company specifically chose not to spend on branding the offerings it developed. This was unfortunate.

The firm was one of the first companies to deliver pagers, and the pagers were of very high quality relative to other existing offerings. However, it would appear that the company believed that product quality should be foremost, and that little branding would be needed if the product quality were highest.

Meanwhile, Motorola specifically focused on innovation *and* branding to support its offerings and today is clearly a communications giant. Yet, at the time when pagers were the breakthrough communications device, many believed that Glenayre truly had a superior offering.

Innovation and branding together make a powerful combination. As Polaroid and Glenayre seemed to show, one competency without the other is seriously problematic.

There are higher tenets than branding

Sergio Zyman is one of the world's most accomplished marketers. He has held senior positions at both Coca-Cola *and* Pepsi. Zyman also built a consulting firm around his expertise. He summarized the purpose of advertising and branding very succinctly in his books, *The End of Advertising as We Know It* and *The End of Marketing as We Know It.*

> *"The only purpose of marketing is to sell more things to more people more often for more money."*

Zyman's quote speaks directly to the appropriate location of branding as Tenet Six and its linkage to the higher tenets in the Return Driven Strategy framework. If the customer doesn't purchase, then the goals of the organization are squandered, regardless of how high brand awareness, brand recognition, or any other similar metric may be. There are higher tenets that branding should be focused on.

Concluding notes on Tenet Six

Society seems to experience tremendous waste when branding activities such as advertising, sales promotions, or other communications can appear dubious in nature or purpose. The branding of an offering that does not fulfill a need or fulfills it relatively inadequately is an incredible drain on the business, on its customers, and on society as a whole. Branding for branding's sake, when there is little focus on the other tenets, can be an incredible waste of attention and resources.

Brands can be extremely valuable to society when they allow people to save time in their need-fulfilling decisions. It's easy to imagine how much time would be wasted if every purchasing decision required the customer to study all available products, test the product's effectiveness, and evaluate all of its supposed attributes.

The value of branding and branding activities is in the time saved by the customer who can quickly understand the offering and the need it fulfills by simply recognizing the brand. When a business brands correctly, it speeds an efficient decision-process, and society as a whole can benefit.

Key Diagnostics for Tenet Six

Do branding initiatives create an indelible connection in the mind of the customer between their explicit understanding of their unmet need and the offering's ability to uniquely fulfill it?

Does the business correctly brand around the offering and not simply the firm?

Are all of the firm's activities around a particular offering consistent with the branding of that offering – and vice versa? Is the branding of the offering consistent with all of the tangible and intangible attributes of the offering?

Are branding activities addressed by far more than advertising, and in some cases possibly remove the need for it?

Are all branding activities conducted within the parameters of and consistent with the higher tenets of strategy?

Does the business use Genuine Assets to better assure achievement of this tenet? Is a process in place for building these Genuine Assets?

Is management continually on the watch for and aware of significant forces of change that could limit the firm's ability to execute on Tenet Six in the future?

Are the right metrics in place and reviewed regularly to help management monitor and communicate the business's ability to execute on Tenet Six? In other words, do the metrics eventually lead to Zyman's goal of "selling more offerings, more often, to more people, at higher prices?"

Harley-Davidson (HOG)

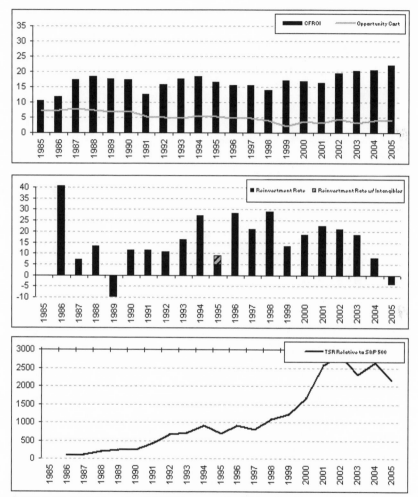

With the genuine asset of an unparalleled brand, Harley-Davidson has built the necessary operational effectiveness and innovation to produce offerings with considerable pricing power. Competing vehicles with similar functional specifications often sell for less than 30% of the price of Harley's branded offering.

This pricing power shines through in high CFROI levels, evident since the early 1980s. By focusing the brand on the baby boomer generation, the growing market carried growing increases in unit sales. In 2004, Harley's valuation fell as its market's growth and investment growth rate fell.

Coca-Cola (KO)

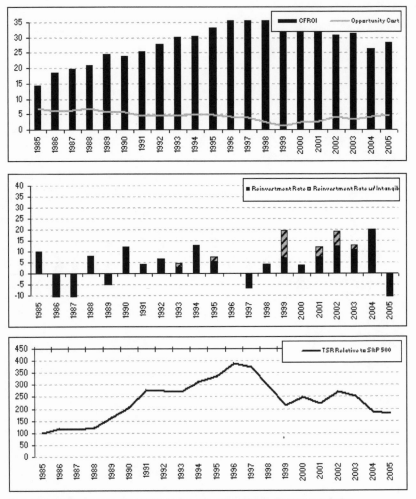

'Brand Offerings' is Tenet Six for a reason. Throughout Coca-Cola's history on this chart, very different CFROI levels appear. Did the CFROI returns rise because the brand suddenly became more valuable, or was something else at work?

In fact, a focus on the other competency tenets, together with the strong brand, represent what drove Coca-Cola's success through the 1990s. This included aggressive partnering arrangements to divest exposure to commodity functions like bottling. Meanwhile, monopolizing the distribution channels like store shelves and vending machines delivered high returns. The brand is powerful, but brand alone is never enough.

Molson Coors (TAP)

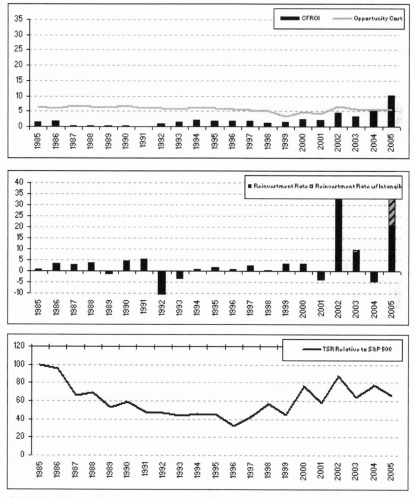

Most of the history of this chart is the history of the Coors Company, formerly the ticker RKY. Over the years, Coors has built a powerful brand, but the organization had been belabored with ineffective supply chain integration and operational ineffectiveness.

Despite CFROI returns at almost zero, well below the cost of capital, the firm increased its asset base, reinvesting in a bad business year after year. Through 1996 the firm showed terrible stock performance because of the mismanagement of returns and growth, regardless of how powerful the brand name. Since 1996, a focus on CFROI improvement has led to notable recovery in valuation.

Abbott Laboratories (ABT)

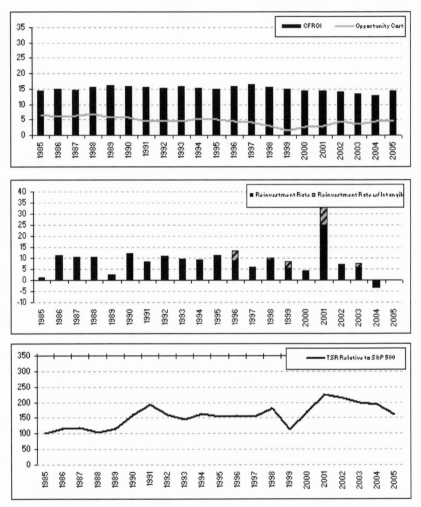

It can be expected that Abbott Labs, as a pharmaceutical firm, would spend extensively on research and development. However, Abbott Labs also spends hundreds of millions of dollars every year in advertising and promotion. For that kind of money, one would think that 'Abbott' would be a household name, but it isn't, with good reason.

Abbott's branding is done properly at the product level, bridging the offering to the need in the mind of the targeted customer. Offering innovation, branding, and effective delivery are reflected in Abbott's CFROI returns, growth rates, and valuation levels.

Part Four

The Supporting Tenets

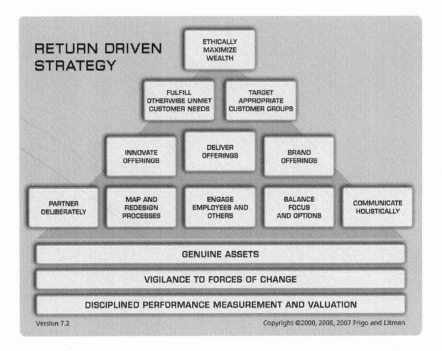

7

Tenet Seven

Partner Deliberately

Tenet Seven is one of the five 'Supporting Tenets' of a Return-Driven organization. These tenets are necessary contributors to high performance, as they support the creation of offerings. Wealth-creating firms plan and perform activities in each of these groups as the higher tenets would dictate.

This tenet, Partner Deliberately, identifies the importance of the disciplined planning of business relationships for driving more effective innovation, branding, and delivery of offerings.

- Consider a wide range of potential partnerships and be creative in developing new types of relationships that can support the competencies of the firm

- Deliberately choose partners based on an assessment of the Genuine Assets brought by each partner and how that can help the firm to build unique offerings as the competency tenets require

- Develop partnership arrangements based on the partner's Genuine Assets and the level of exclusivity needed

- Be vigilant to forces of change that continually affect the Genuine Assets of the partners and the types and nature of partnering relationships that are available

- Create performance measures that bring incentives to the partners that support the business strategy. Value the monetary aspect of partner relationships based on the long-term impact that those partnerships will have on cash flow streams

Partnering with purpose

Any successful business leverages the partnership of a whole cast of players outside the firm. The right partnerships allow the business to focus on its strengths and rely on others to do things it ought not bother. The strongest partnerships bring unique assets together that allow the firm to innovate, brand, and deliver unique need-fulfilling offerings

The decisions behind any partnering activity should be driven by the higher six tenets. Partnerships that are formed indiscriminately are ones that don't follow the higher guidelines.

Poor returns follow companies that partner for reasons that don't support the higher tenets. There seem to be many reasons that businesses enter into deep partnering arrangements that have little purpose. Sometimes firms feel they must make acquisitions because the competitors are doing so, or enter into outsourcing arrangements because another firm has extolled its benefits.

Seeing a full spectrum of partnerships

Partnerships range from being very open to very exclusive. On the open side, partnerships could include basic arm's length transactional relationships. More exclusive partnerships would include legal joint ventures between two firms.

The following are examples of the most open forms of partnering (so open, one might not refer to them as 'partnerships' at all):

- Basic vendor-customer models
- Bid-ask models or auctions
- Simple buy/sell transactions

Partnership arrangements with tighter relationships being developed between the parties could be:

- Industry mutuals
- Long-term outsourcing arrangements
- Shared intellectual capital
- Licensing arrangements

These would be the most exclusive partnerships (relationships that involve controlling interests):

- Joint ventures
- Partial ownership stakes, minority interests
- Exclusive license contracts
- Outright mergers and acquisitions

When partnering, management must believe that the relationship has a specific purpose that fulfills the higher tenets.

- The pharmaceutical giants Takeda and Abbot might form TAP in order to leverage each other's sales distribution networks. The clear reason is to provide consumers with drugs they would not otherwise be able to get as efficiently as through the TAP partnership.

- After its debacle in attempting to build its own online business, Toys R Us partnered with Amazon.com to help it find efficient ways of supplying its toys to consumers over the Internet.

- Insurance companies in the utility energy created a mutual consortium for re-insuring them, spreading their risks across a large group.

How exclusive, and when?

The right level of partnering depends on the importance of the partner's assets in the creation of a unique offering for achieving the unmet needs of targeted markets. If the partner's assets are only marginally essential to the offering's creation, then more open partner-ships are in order. If the partner's assets are absolutely essential, then more exclusive partnerships are necessary to ensure the strategy's longer-term viability.

As an example, consider a software company and the programmers designing the software. The management of employee benefits plans is necessary to do business. However, one would not consider benefits administration as a genuine asset necessary for inducing employees to design better software. The benefits may be key, but not the admini-stration of them. Hewitt Associates and other firms have grown sizeable outsourcing businesses by taking advantage of this. Firms smartly outsource their administration so they can focus on the real Genuine Assets of their particular strategy.

Partnering in the right part of the spectrum

Deliberately choosing the best type of partnership is based on:

1) The ability to enhance the activities designed for achiev-ing the higher tenets

2) The need for exclusivity in the partnership given the im-portance to the potential uniqueness of the offerings, in other words, the Genuine Assets of the partner

When the wrong level of partnering is chosen

There are times that industries go through periods of believing that 'vertical integration' is key to success. Essentially, the business feels that to survive and succeed, it needs to actually own all of the inputs and all of the distribution of a particular offering. The chain would extend by owning everything from sourcing of raw materials all the way down to the distributors of the product.

During the 1980s, The Coors Company, makers of one of the more popular lines of beer in the United States, felt that vertical integration was important. The firm bought up canning companies. The firm also bought aluminum manufacturing businesses, naturally, because cans are made of aluminum.

One needs to ask the question… can aluminum containers be manufactured so uniquely that they would cause a customer to purchase that can of beer, and pass up all competing brands? Could the aluminum itself that is in the can be made with such singular precision that people would buy Coors beer because of that particular aluminum quality, unparalleled by others?

If the answer to both of those questions is "no," then there is one explanation for the poor returns experienced by the Coors company over decades.

One can contrast this with Coca-Cola during the same time period. The firm did exactly the opposite of vertical integration. Instead, the beverage maker made great strides in divesting itself of bottling operations. It certainly never became a glass or aluminum manufacturer. The firm retained equity interests in businesses in order to retain control over bottling. Focusing on the marketing and branding of its offerings, and monopolizing control over key distribution assets. Coca-Cola's returns rose year after year for more than a decade.

Acquisitions and growth

There are many corporate examples of poor-performing returns where unnecessary acquisitions have been repeatedly made out of management's desire to simply be a larger business. In part, this can be traced to compensation programs that excessively reward increased revenue generation as opposed to cash flow generation above the cost of capital.

Acquisitions can be seen as a quick fix to achieving sales growth or earnings growth. Managers can feel they would be 'left behind' when they see competitors acquiring. When asked about the purpose of a sizable merger, employees, middle management, and even the bankers have been often heard to cite a reason for the merger as the following:

"Senior management wants this deal to happen."

No one wants to question upper management, and often lots of reasons are quoted such as "earnings accretion" or "multiple expansion" with no grounding in cash flows or valuations as investors would see. These deals don't necessarily lead to higher returns, and often do the opposite. Many studies have shown that a majority of acquiring firms tend to *lose value* when making major acquisitions, regardless of what "earnings growth" may have been achieved.

When another firm has Genuine Assets that could be combined to create a more unique offering, an acquisition is in order. But for various parts of a business, there are always some functions that, while important, could be done better by someone else. That may naturally lead to a smaller firm, but could be the right path to higher returns.

The competencies as compasses

In the early 2000s, a management team at a national commercial bank was asked by upper management to investigate partnership with one of the leading Internet portals. It appeared that competitor banks were striking deals with the portals, and managers worried that their firm might be left out of the action. The potential deal was sought with one of Yahoo, America Online, or Microsoft's msn.com. Discussions with all three were quickly under way.

Managers asked them the right question,

> *"Could a partnership with a leading Internet search engine lead to a new offering that fulfills otherwise unmet needs of the bank's customers or potential customers?"*

Six weeks into the analysis, management decided that no major partnership would be struck. There simply was no need. The Return Driven Strategy framework was used as a tool for evaluating the initiative. If the partnership made sense, it would have supported the competency tenets in some way.

Viewed through Tenet Four, Deliver Offerings:

At that time, no one could conceive how this portal partnership would lead to more efficient or more effective delivery of product. Could checks be processed or cleared faster, or loans processed faster with the portals in the way the bank was already doing with its internal eBusiness initiatives? The answer from the managers was "Doubtful."

Viewed through Tenet Five, Innovate Offerings:

In brainstorming sessions, no new Internet-based bank products were envisioned *that were not already in development.* By the early 2000s, all the banks already had web-based banking offerings such as online bill pay services, or were far into their development.

Viewed through Tenet Six, Brand Offerings:

The managers discussed the bank's desire to reach the portals' customers. They realized that what was being considered was essentially advertising through the portal, *not branding with it.* They decided that it would be difficult to believe that customers would have more faith and comfort in placing their savings accounts or home loans in the hands of 'AOL Lending' or 'Microsoft Bank.' While the major search engines and portals have come a long way in confidence-building, at the time this type of branding was not desirable by the bank managers.

None of the Competency Tenets could be used to justify a more exclusive relationship such as a joint venture. The negotiations to create an exclusive partnership discontinued, naturally, as one was not justifiable based on the above analysis.

Concluding notes on Tenet Seven

When firms fail to build the right relationships and partnerships, they hinder the competencies of innovation, branding, and delivery. But partner, they must. The poet John Donne wrote, "No man is an island, entire of itself; every man is a piece of the continent." Similarly, no business can survive, let alone succeed, without carefully leveraging the assets and activities of others.

Sometimes companies strive to do everything themselves, integrating too many parts of their business elements under one roof. Often, they find them slow to innovate offerings or unable to reach customers adequately once offerings are created.
On the other hand, some firms attempt to enter into more exclusive relationships in unnecessary areas. The managers find them focused on

growth initiatives that are dubious in nature. Chances of achieving higher returns become slim.

The driving motivation behind all partnering activities should be the promise of better innovating, branding, or delivering offerings. What is the benefit to society of partnering deliberately? If followed, it means higher returns for all the constituents of the firm, and thereby higher benefit to society as resources are not wasted on unnecessary activities.

Key Diagnostics for Tenet Seven

Is a full spectrum of partnering arrangements considered when creating and evaluating the business's relationships with other firms?

Are less exclusive relationships sought when the partner is not central to the uniqueness of the firm's offerings, and more exclusive relationships when the partner is necessary to do so?

Are the Genuine Assets of each side of a partnership considered in determining the right partner and the right type of partnership?

Are all partnerships focused on improving the firm's ability to innovate, brand, and deliver offerings to fulfill otherwise unmet needs of the appropriate customer groups?

Are all partnership activities performed consistently and within the parameters of the higher tenets?

Does the business use Genuine Assets to better assure achievement of this tenet? Is a process in place for building these Genuine Assets?

Is management continually on the watch for and aware of significant forces of change that could limit the firm's ability to execute on Tenet Seven in the future?

Are the right metrics in place and reviewed regularly to help management monitor and communicate the business's ability to execute on Tenet Seven?

Danaher Corp (DHR)

With DBS, the Danaher Business System, the company is able to take smaller manufacturing companies that are not performing well and turn around their operations and CFROI levels. The firm could do this on a consultative basis, but to enjoy the highest return for their work, Danaher acquires these firms outright, and then enjoys the full cash flow benefits of the improved performance.

This, in turn, creates an incredible growth rate for Danaher, that, with the CFROI level, has yielded a stock that has risen more than 12 times the market average.

Systeme Anwendungen Produkte (SAP)

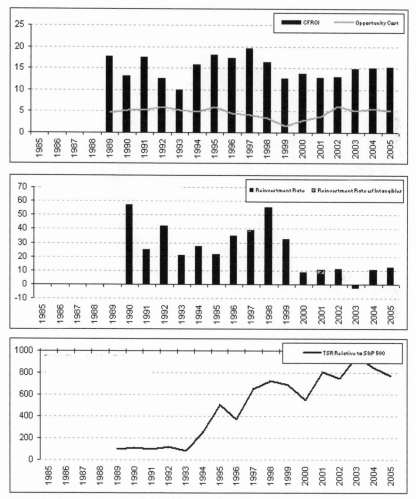

SAP's focus on ERP software (Enterprise Resource Planning) gave it a target customer base of every medium to large company in the world. Firms can spend tens if not hundreds of millions on SAP installations. To accomplish this, SAP partnered aggressively with multiple consulting firms, as the consulting firms were advising companies on how to integrate their various IT systems.

For installation, the consultants would receive the hourly fees, while SAP received an ongoing annuity from the company for the software because once an ERP system is installed, switching costs are very high. The result: the largest software company in Europe, with high CFROI returns, growth, and shareholder value creation.

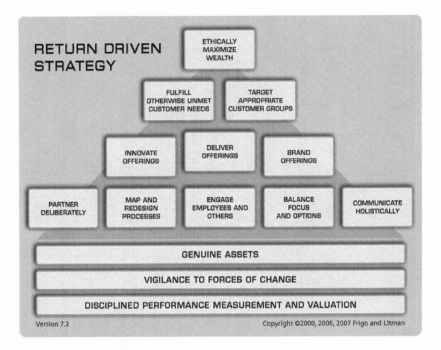

Tenet Eight

Map and Redesign Processes

Tenet Eight is one of the five 'Supporting Tenets' of a return-driven organization. The key to redesigning any process is to understand its purpose and change or develop processes to achieve that focus.

- Determine the processes that are necessary to support all of the higher tenets of business strategy. Be sure to go beyond internal processes and pay attention to important processes of customers, key partners, and others

- Map those processes, focusing on the inputs and the outputs, and the exchanges that occur from resources used toward need fulfillment

- When mapping and redesigning processes, keep the *context* of the process in mind, being careful not to overly focus on the specific content of the activity

- Employ Genuine Assets that provide an ability to map and redesign processes in ways others cannot replicate

- Be vigilant to forces of change that continually affect the context and the content of each process, sometimes requiring abandonment of a process altogether

- Create performance measures that allow processes to be managed toward the higher tenets of business strategy

Mapping precedes navigation

If managers took their lead from sailors, they would never set out without a map. Yet, managers invariably neglect to take the time to map key aspects of the business. Maps allow managers to consciously note critical inputs, activities, outputs, and dependencies.

The mapping exercise itself has many benefits. Foremost of which is an ability to move away from the content of specific activities into the context of why they are performed. Managers will seek to do things better, but don't always realize how the firm and its constituents might prosper by doing something radically different. Great mapping is the beginning of great navigation, and a precursor to great strategy.

When to map

Many times, part of the value provided by management consultants is simply helping the management team to realize the importance of a particular activity. When problems arise in a business, it can be easy to focus on fixing the wrong things. The symptoms may be seen as the problem, and the problem may go unnoticed. If critical changes in a business are being considered, mapping the existing activities is the first order of the day, to determine not only if, but also to what extent, changes are necessary.

Even in simple businesses, members of a management team could assume that everyone understands the issues of the business similarly. However, perception is a frail thing, and each person's explicitly stated perspective can help to form a more accurate mosaic of the total issue.

What is it that customers really value? What are the critical bottlenecks in the firm's processes? Certainly, management teams don't need consultants to ask the questions necessary to map their processes. However, having an outsider, even someone simply from a different area of the firm, can help to facilitate open discourse. The physical mapping helps to ground everyone, and raise issues before strategic initiatives are begun.

Identifying and framing business problems accurately is the first step to solving them. In fact, proper framing of the problem may be most of the effort in figuring out the solution.

One need not wait for the problem

Being aware of the current state of the business is important, and management should not wait for a problem to arise before adequately mapping it. The map changes the entire platform for better planning and improving the business. There are tremendous benefits from a conscious examination of dependencies and motivations of the important constituents of the business.

What to map

Who are the key constituents of the business, and what are the key exchanges between them?

- Identify the important groups of a focused area of the business. This could be investors, customers, employee groups, suppliers, partners, or others

- Specifically identify the exchanges of cash flows. For what exactly is the cash being exchanged, in terms of product, service, or psychological value?

- Strive to understand the needs that are being fulfilled in each exchange on both sides of the exchange, and how well

- Identify the key influences in the exchange; what actually prompts the exchange to happen?

- How are prices and payments determined in each exchange? Are prices determined closer to the value of the offering to the party making the payment, or based on the costs incurred by the party developing it?

- What networks are already in place around exchanges and transactions, and who are the key influencers?

- In each exchange, identify two key parties at a time, drawing simple arrows between them, identifying the above exchanges and what drives them.

Why?

An effective exercise is 'Why-axis analysis.' It's a pun based on the 'y' axis of a Cartesian plane, where 'Y' is the 'up' axis. Simply ask 'why'something occurs in a transaction, and whatever the answer, ask 'why' again and again. At some point, a better identification of the true reasons for the exchange may be reached. Many times, the ultimate reasons behind every exchange center on some basic human need, such as those in Maslow's Hierarchy of human needs.

Improving *your* pyramid by understanding *others'*

Each of the characteristics for mapping should sound familiar. In total, they describe the top tenets of the Return Driven Strategy framework. This mapping should not stop with the processes specific to the business but move beyond the immediate doors.

- What are the key exchanges around the business's most important customers?
- What are those surrounding the most important vendors? Each has its own 'pyramid' of strategy, so to speak.
- Who are your customers' customers? Who are your suppliers' suppliers? What makes them all tick?

A lack of understanding of these issues leads to blind planning and false senses of direction. Just as businesses and business cycles can model human behavior, it's not ironic that a more total awareness of the business's place in its community is necessary for business success.

After the map, when to redesign it

The higher tenets should drive the decision to redesign a particular process. The question should not be as simple as, "How much can the process be improved?" The firm could have the greatest process in the world for making buggy whips, but no one will buy them if the need is not there.

More important is to understand what the potential impact will be on the cash flow returns of the business and the potential need fulfillment of its constituents. There are no inherently good, bad, lucky, or unlucky areas of a process to redesign. The main focus is on the potential positive impact on achieving the higher tenets.

Redesigning to improve operations

In the 1980s and 1990s, Coca-Cola took steps to focus on the highly valuable areas of the processes between production and final consumption. It held onto the most valuable processes, and divested or outsourced as much of everything else as possible. Undoubtedly, this was no accident as the firm realized the non-value-adding areas of its operations, divesting itself of those aspects of its business.

Dell is a more recent example of the benefits of redesigning processes in a similar fashion. While the products may be different, the business model is extremely similar to Coca-Cola's. Over the years, Dell continued to outsource the manufacturing of its laptops and desktops to other partners. They found that the value in their business stemmed not from the creation of the computer, but in allowing the customers to customize it for them, with a myriad of options. At the time, this was something with which no in-store sales could compete. Many other computer manufacturers did not want to anger there in-store selling partners, and so were late to re-create the same business model.

Some managers make the following statement about their suppliers:

> *"The main focus of our suppliers is being profitable, but we want the cheapest prices possible. We're at natural odds."*

Meanwhile the suppliers can reflect that statement, expressing this:

> *"The main focus of our business customers is profitability. The higher prices we charge them, the lower their returns, so all we can do is compromise."*

In Dell's case, the firm believed that its manufacturing partners could produce many parts of the computer far cheaper than Dell could itself. In that case, it was smart to give those producers more and more of that operation. This in turn allowed the firm to focus on the areas in which it had gained competitive advantages, in the Dell Direct model.

Two can win at this game

There are many examples of partnerships where both the supplying firm and the retailer have high returns. While Wal-Mart has high returns, not all of its vendors suffer as the press would show. Many of the high return businesses mentioned throughout this book have significant revenues through goods sold through Wal-Mart, and yet still enjoy high returns as well.

Both the supplying and the purchasing business can profit, if the processes are redesigned appropriately, and each business focuses on its respective core strengths in producing a unique offering that fulfills an unmet need. If that is accomplished, there will be more than enough cash to split among the parties.

Redesigning to innovate

Dell's direct-to-customer model has also made a great example of mapping and redesigning processes. It shows how a firm could innovate the offering by focusing on the totality of the customer experience. The process of purchasing a computer is as much a part of the offering as the computer itself. Before Dell, the process of buying a computer had been quite similar across the industry.

The sales process

When mapping the customer sales experience, a natural bottleneck can exist. That is, the salesperson.

Customers encounter a salesperson and often have a natural aversion toward purchase, hesitant to disclose their true needs. Whether in real estate, home electronics, or hiring consultants, there is a natural well-founded fear that the salesperson may attempt to sell the customer more than what the customer needs. This issue becomes painfully evident when a salesperson approaches a potential customer and says "Can I help you?" The most common customer response,

"I'm just looking."

That statement is made by customers even when they are desperately in need of a product or service, and prepared to immediately buy. The Dell Direct model allowed more savvy customers to explore the computer purchase without the presence of the salesperson. Not only did this knock-out a costly aspect of the exchange, the middleman, but it also changed the nature of the offering entirely. Purchasing a computer through a salesperson is a *different offering* to the customers, not just a different sales channel, changing the experience of the process dramatically.

Consider two types of transactions. In the first, customers purchase and choose a product through a salesperson who has a fixed set of offerings, such as buying a computer at a store. In the other transaction, a website allows customers to self-select from a myriad of offerings, and can deliberate, unhampered by the pressure of the salesperson.

With the barrier of sales pressure gone, the customer is free to purchase at will, and may even choose to purchase more features than if a salesperson tried to "upsell." These early findings identify the salesperson-bottleneck issue in some types of purchasing processes. With no bottleneck, exchanges can flow more freely as need-fulfillment can be sought more openly and willingly.

Redesigning the customers' processes, not overly focusing on the firm's

The advent of the Internet and the World Wide Web allowed for a number of new business models to come about. What was found was that the key tenets of business strategy held, whether in the new economy or the old one. INSWEB is a case in point.

Many different types of insurance policies exist: car insurance, home insurance, insurance of personal valuables such as watches or jewelry, and on and on. INSWEB noticed this issue and thought that with the

Web, a one-stop shop of insurance could be made. Therefore, when people think about insurance, they would think of INSWEB. Few people reading this would recall INSWEB right now, and with good reason.

INSWEB can be applauded for its attempt to redesign the purchasing process, but its focus was not squarely on the mind of the customer seeking to be insured. INSWEB was unsuccessful in its attempt to fulfill an unmet need. The need did not exist as they had perceived it.

As one might surmise, people do not think about insurance as an isolated subject. Instead, people tend to think about car insurance when they buy a car. They think about home insurance when they buy a home. They tend to think about life insurance and disability insurance after getting married or having children.

A portal aggregating insurance products of different types doesn't fit within the customer's natural processes. Further, some insurance types are extremely complex and/or extremely personal. One might share personal information on car insurance over the web, but may be more reluctant for other types of insurance.

And so, a one-stop shop for insurance might have made sense from an industry or vendor standpoint, but not from a customer standpoint. Many firms have done extremely well by offering their insurance products over the web, but they have remained focused on the way the customer thinks. With ten years of publicly available information, from 1998 to 2007, INSWEB's CFROI levels have never been above zero.

Redesigning the offering to save time and money

Wal-Mart was able to redesign the exchanges in retail in many different ways. One example is Wal-Mart's strategy to provide the vital few offerings people need most instead of the costly many.

Focusing on customer buying patterns, Wal-Mart realized how much consumers value time and convenience. In many departments, such as toys, Wal-Mart carries far fewer selections of products than its competitors. Instead, it focuses on the products in demand.

Customers are loathe to park their vehicles at one store, shop, get back in their car, drive to another store, park and shop again, and so on. Wal-Mart has focused on having the 20% of goods that sell 80% of the time. When coupled with prices as low as or lower than other retailers, the convenience of a smaller 'most popular' selection overwhelms the need for an exhaustive selection. This has resulted in customers by-passing the inconvenience in visiting several stores, and focusing so much of their purchases on one, Wal-Mart.

Redesigning to improve the brand

Firms like Wal-Mart and Home Depot have done a great job of redes-igning processes. They have created one-stop super centers, remarkably innovating the customer's experience and buying pattern. They've done so well that the firms' suppliers, the actual manufactur-ers of many of the goods sold in those stores, have encountered issues in their own business models.

Many original manufacturers have exclaimed similarly:

> *"The distributor has garnered so much of the business; they are able to apply undue pressure on us."*

Of course they do. As cost reduction is a key aspect of the end cus-tomer's reason to purchase, the big retailers have sought to deliver what the customer wants. That means lower payments to the manufac-turers. However, this misses an incredibly important point of the exchange. Customers purchase for more reasons than price.

Many firms have succeeded against the big retailers by recognizing this issue and focusing their efforts around it. These manufacturers parry and deflect those pressures, building suitable exchanges in which both succeed. Cash flow returns can remain high at both if the final customers get more of what they want as well.

In 1999, a now infamous letter from Home Depot was sent to most if not all of its suppliers. Home Depot feared what the Internet could do. Could each manufacturer develop a direct model in the same way Dell had with its computer offerings? Every big retailer had to ask this question during the late 1990s.

So, Home Depot leveraged what power it could, telling its manufacturers that it would look very sorely on any manufacturer attempting to go direct to the end customer. In essence, going direct would make the vendor a competitor and Home Depot could respond by being "...hesitant to do business with its competitors." For fear of losing the significant sales it had through the retailing giant, many manufacturers had to consider their work carefully.

One primary equipment manufacturer of home-building supplies received the letter, but continued to build out its web-based operations. The large manufacturer did not actually sell to the buyers of its products directly, but it continued to *market to them directly.* The manufacturer's CFO stated bluntly:

> *"Home Depot is playing a game of chicken and many manufacturers will have to back down. The ultimate buyers of our products are well-aware of our unique quality by name. The absence of our products in Home Depot's store would strongly impact the image of Home Depot itself."*

The firm continued to build out its online initiatives, regardless of Home Depot's threat. It felt that its focus not only on the quality of the offering, but also on the end-customer's awareness of that fact, brought parity to the discussions with the super-retailer. Were they right?

Years later, these particular building supplies continue to be sold prominently in Home Depot stores. The vendor's focus on the customer side of the exchange was essential to its survival and its success.

Concluding notes on Tenet Eight

Better maps, better planning, superior navigation. When redesigning the process, return-driven managers strive to relinquish attachment to previously held ideals. Too often people hold on to tradition simply because of inertia.

Just because an activity has been done a certain way for decades does not mean that it needs to continue to be done that same way in the future. By rearranging processes, realigning relationships, redefining and better understanding needs, managers can find new ways of fulfilling otherwise unmet needs, or the needs of far larger groups of customers.

While there is power in this tenet, one must realize that the map is not the territory, it's just the map. It can be helpful as a representation of the business, but care must be taken to question it regularly, challenging assumptions from various perspectives.

Yet, the mapping itself can create great changes in a business. This thinking is rooted in many different disciplines. An "observer effect" is noted in physics and social sciences. Dr. Wayne Dyer, the popular self-development author and speaker states it elegantly,

> *"When you change the way you look at things, the things you look at change."*

The observer has as much to do with the perception of reality as does the observed. Successful firms better understand the key exchanges between their constituents and the core reasons for why the exchanges occur. They seek to better understand unmet needs and how to better fulfill them, examining the entirety of the offering and not simply the functional aspects of it.

Key Diagnostics for Tenet Eight

Have all key nodes and constituents of the business model been identified, along with key exchanges of cash flow for need-fulfillment?

Are the processes of new initiatives mapped as part of the new business or product evaluation process? Is the totality of the customer experience considered, and the processes of the constituents and not just the firm's?

Are all mapping and redesign activities performed consistently and within the parameters of the higher tenets?

Does the business use Genuine Assets to better assure achievement of this tenet? Is a process in place for building these Genuine Assets?

Is management continually on the watch for and aware of significant forces of change that could limit the firm's ability to execute on this tenet in the future?

Are the right metrics in place and reviewed regularly to help management monitor and communicate the business's ability to execute on this tenet?

Dell Inc (DELL)

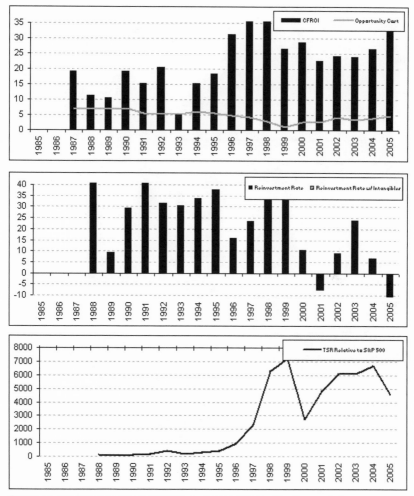

Few may realize how Dell has mapped and redesigned both the output and *input* sides of its processes. The Dell direct model was revolutionary, as it leveraged the Internet to allow customers' purchasing process to include personal customization of computers. On the supply side, Dell aggressively turned over manufacturing of the PCs to other companies, changing the processes in ways that support the mass customization model.

The redesigned processes created a business that has never shown a low CFROI return. Since 2001, growth has slowed as markets became saturated and so the stock price stopped rising. Yet, the CFROI levels remain as high as ever.

157

General Growth Properties (GGP)

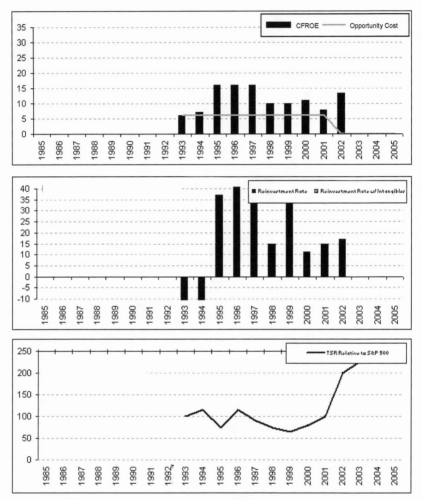

General Growth Properties is a Real Estate Investment Trust specializing in owning and managing over 200 malls. Once, the center of town served as people's main community center. GGP has been aware of the changing demographics and lifestyles and how people's processes for shopping and running errands have changed.

The firm has focused its malls on becoming life centers, with services and offerings not common to malls in the past such as upscale restaurants and varied entertainment options. While real estate cycles can fluctuate heavily, GGP has garnered high CFROE returns and growth rates with out-sized stock market performance.

DRIVEN

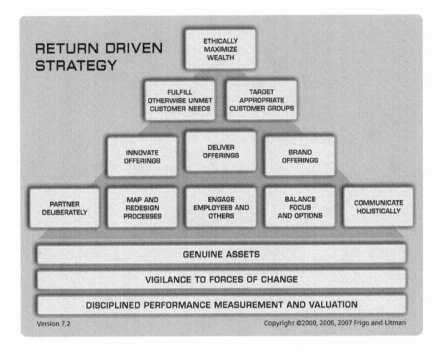

Tenet Nine

Engage Employees and Others

Tenet Nine is one of the five 'Supporting Tenets.' High-performance firms treat their employees like customers, understanding exactly what services they would like to receive from employees, and designing incentive systems that fulfill employees' needs in order to get those services. In the tenet, the word, 'others,' refers to other individuals who may not be employees of the firm, but are critical to its success. These may include independent contractors, the personnel at vendors, distributors, or other partners of the business, throughout its various processes.

- Before embarking on any type of employee-related program, determine the types and nature of services needed from employees in order to achieve the higher tenets

- Just as if one were targeting the appropriate customer groups, determine what types of employees would be most likely to be able to provide the services the firm needs given its required competencies and goals

- Realize the existence of the complete end-to-end employee life cycle, including firm awareness and recruiting at one end and alumni or even customer status at the other end of the cycle

- Create incentives, compensation plans, and other offerings throughout the entire employee life cycle that will create *employee engagement* toward the firm's goals

- Realize that monetary compensation is only one aspect of employee engagement, and without others, can be incredibly ineffective

- Employ Genuine Assets that provide the firm with unique incentives as a means for finding the right employees and engaging them in ways others cannot replicate

- Be vigilant to forces of change that affect the entirety of the employee life cycle. Stay aware of what motivates employees to provide the services that changing strategies require

- Create performance measures that are aligned with the achievement of the higher tenets

Thinking of employees as customers

Companies succeed when employees and other individuals are aligned with the organization's goals in creating and delivering the offerings that fulfill customers' unmet needs. To accomplish this, individuals need to be engaged.

Just as each business has a pyramid of wealth-creation, individuals each have their own definitions of wealth and their own 'pyramids.' Firms with the highest levels of returns build offerings for employees that help them to fulfill their unmet needs. Employees provide their time and effort in exchange for what the firm offers them, something that includes compensation, but requires more than that.

No alignment and misalignment

Is this tenet placed 'so low' in the hierarchy of the pyramid because employees are less important? On the contrary, the right employees in the right roles become Genuine Assets to the firm's plans and implementations, necessary to driving high return businesses.

From a planning perspective, however, it's important to first determine what types of offerings will be needed and for what customers, followed by hiring the right types of employees and engaging them in ways that promote the building of those offerings.

In other words, a business with the best employees producing incredibly well-built products will still experience low returns if no customers buy the products. So a key question may be, "Who are the right employees and how should we pay them?" The answers come from a thorough planning of the higher tenets.

Bad strategy drives bad employee management

It would be difficult to over emphasize the importance of getting the top tenets right, before recruiting, hiring, and engaging employees.

One management team misunderstood how stock markets value companies. They mistakenly believed that near-term quarterly revenue and earnings estimates were the primary drivers of the market's valuations of the firm. That belief permeated the firm's ranks. One senior vice-president running a large project thought that if his team could reach certain billing milestones by the quarter's end, they could impact the revenues reported for the firm. This in turn would allow the company to reach the forecasted quarterly estimates.

With this in mind, the manager drove everyone on the project to work extremely long days, nights, and weekends. He was devoted to the 'big push' to the end of the quarter. He was successful in his short-term goal. Because of that major project, the firm reached billing levels and revenues that were in line with estimates.

Of course, that type of 'push' on employees has other ramifications. Some employees, very talented ones, quit immediately after and some during that project. And, while the company met its revenues for that period, the stock still fell based on the longer-term prospects of the firm, not the short-term revenue management. So, not only did that quarter not save the company's stock price, the 'push' sacrificed longer-term prospects by losing great employees unnecessarily.

Best place, but for what type of employee?

There are many different company studies with lots of press and fanfare that rank the 'best companies' for employees to work. Many times rankings are based upon benefits and compensation studies, or along employee work and lifestyles. However, these types of studies become problematic, and may cause a firm to target employee engagement in a vacuum, devoid of linkage to the overall strategy of the business. All employees are not created equal, and employees with different skill-sets and personalities will apply different values to the same benefit, environment, or even compensation level.

During the periods leading up to the late 1990s, both Charles Schwab and Merrill Lynch exhibited very high cash flow returns. Both financial services firms enjoyed high stock price valuations as well. Both firms received accolades for being best places to work in one study or another. However, the differences between the firms were stark.

Merrill's reputation as a typical Wall Street firm was directly counter to Charles Schwab which was termed the 'Anti-Wall Street' brokerage. Brokers at Merrill were paid by commissions, whereas Schwab employees were salaried with a bonus. Even the geographical differences help to describe how the firms' cultures differed, with Merrill based in New York and Schwab in San Francisco. Yet, both firms received rankings as best places to work.

The key question is, "Best place for whom?" Can one imagine how dramatically different the experience would be if Merrill's and Schwab's employees were to switch places in terms of location, lifestyle, and compensation? What's best for one employee is not what's best for another. It's not about hiring the 'best' employee; it's about creating the 'best fit' given the types of employees required. Both Merrill and Schwab generated high cash flow returns and valuations throughout the periods described.

While employees clearly require some level of monetary compensation, seldom is this enough to generate the type of engagement that propels firms into the highest levels of cash flow performance. In fact, the highest levels of cash flow driving employee performance stem from non-monetary sources. And it should go without saying that non-monetary means of motivation contribute even further to monetary success.

Best employee for what place?

The following statement is heard regularly by managers when recruiting for their firms:

"We look to hire the best and the brightest."

The phrase is simply a cliché, and it's generally not meant to carry much weight as it can refer to the general hiring practices of an entire firm. However, a problem occurs when the description for the hiring and recruiting of candidates goes no deeper. In worst circumstances, the cliché serves as a placeholder even when describing the right candidate for a particular job. Often, this is because a more specific description of the ideal candidate has not been thought out in alignment with the role of that candidate in the firm's overall strategy.

Should a business hire detailed-oriented people or big thinkers? Expressive personalities or analytical? Creative thinkers or task-oriented project managers? Just as one employer could be great for one person, but terrible for another, so could an *employee* be perfect for one firm, and a terrible fit elsewhere. The key imitative for the firm is to first determine what type of employee is needed, long before developing a strategy for recruiting, hiring, or compensating.

Employees should be thought of like customers. But instead of exchanging cash for products and services, employees provide their time and effort for the right employment offering.

- What kinds of skills and services are required from employees in order to innovate, brand, and deliver unique offerings?

- What employment offering can be provided to create high engagement from the right employees who can provide those skills and services?

Segment, target, and position

Great marketers understand the importance of knowing how to segment customer groups along traits of like need, target the right groups, and position offerings in ways that can generate interest and purchases.

Return-driven firms apply this methodology to the recruiting and hiring side of the business as well. *The same skills found in a great marketing department are found in the skills of a great human resources department.*

Employee related efforts should mirror strategic marketing. Once strategies for the higher tenets have been determined, return-driven businesses consider what the attributes of the right employees are, and then segment, target, and position employee groups and offerings to attract and engage the right employees and individuals, before and after hiring.

The right offering for the right employee

Paychex is a firm that has experienced incredibly high corporate returns and growth rates for over two decades. In designing their payroll processing offering for small-to-medium sized businesses, the firm wanted to match up employees that could better fit with the target customers. For years, it by-passed a focus on prominent business schools and sought to hire the highest level candidates from community colleges. That employment strategy became part of their culture.

The firm's employment offering in terms of compensation, benefits, and lifestyle could be positioned as incredibly compelling to students from community colleges. It made Paychex one of the most sought after firms by those targeted employee groups. Low employee turnover, higher job satisfaction – and higher cash flow returns – were the result. Had the company targeted the larger, 'brand name' business schools for those roles, Paychex's employment offering might not have been as differentiated and enviable.

People have their own "pyramids"

People do what they are paid to do, but they are 'paid' by much more than just monetary compensation. Once ideal employee segments have been determined, successful businesses consider the following:

- How do the employees define wealth them?
- What are their otherwise unmet needs?
- How would they prefer to innovate their skills and build their own reputations to achieve their goals of wealth-creation?

The above questions apply a Return Driven Strategy pyramid to the individual's career. Each employee perceives an individual set of personal needs and an idea of wealth, which differs from person to person. Through innovation, reputation-building, and delivery of their individual service offering as employees (their own personal competency tenets), they fulfill the need of their customer (their employer). The more the employer needs that particular employee's offering, and the more unique that offering is, the higher the compensation.

High-performance firms understand commonalities of targeted and existing potential employees. This understanding allows the firm to shape the employment offering in ways that fit how the employees define wealth, particularly in ways beyond compensation.

In recent years, the expression, 'mass customization,' has labeled the efforts of firms to design products and services that are incredibly individualized for customers, but in ways that require low resources of the business. The same concept can be applied to employees.

When possible, employers can individualize the employment offering, while still gaining the services, efforts, and overall culture required to achieve the higher tenets. Allowing individuals to customize their benefits package is a step in the right direction, but one might consider a more comprehensive framework for understanding what motivates the employee.

A framework for employee engagement

Any successful firm seeks employees that are engaged – a state where people take ownership over what they do and actively strive to help the business achieve its objectives. One framework studied and promoted by the consulting firm of Hewitt Associates focuses on seven 'levers,' of which only one is compensation-based:

- Compensation and benefits
- Culture and purpose
- Work activities
- Relationships
- Leadership
- Quality of life
- Opportunity

In fact, Hewitt contends that at best, monetary compensation can only be 'non-negative.' In other words, a business can pay people too little and gain less engagement from employees or fail to hire the right ones in the first place. However, if a firm overpays, they don't generate over-work or over-effort. Instead, other factors beyond compensation tend to drive the right employment packages.

Concluding notes on Tenet Nine

There is a total shift in thinking when a firm sees employees and other individuals important to the firm as customers. It brings the entire concept of great marketing strategy to bear on superior hiring.

High-performing firms find them not only fulfilling the needs of customers, but fulfilling the needs of employees and other individuals on route to achieving that end. These firms then generate high cash flow returns for investors. All three constituents win.

Key Diagnostics for Tenet Nine

Have the top six tenets of business strategy been determined adequately prior to designing and executing any employee recruiting, hiring, or compensation strategies?

Given the types of employees and requisite skill sets required to achieve the objectives of the top six tenets, is the employee offering designed to motivate in ways beyond simply compensation (all seven levers of employee engagement, for instance)?

Have the employees' personal pyramids been considered, and does the firm have flexibility to customize its employment offering to create engagement?

Does the firm have the controls and culture in place to ensure that the business avoids any gross unethical conduct against the employees?

Does management plan around the entire end-to-end life cycle of an employee consistently and within the parameters of the higher tenets?

Does the business use Genuine Assets to better assure achievement of this tenet? Is a process in place for building these Genuine Assets?

Is management continually on the watch for and aware of significant forces of change that could limit the firm's ability to execute on this tenet in the future?

Are the right metrics in place and reviewed regularly to help management monitor and communicate the business's ability to execute on this tenet?

Charles Schwab (SCHW)

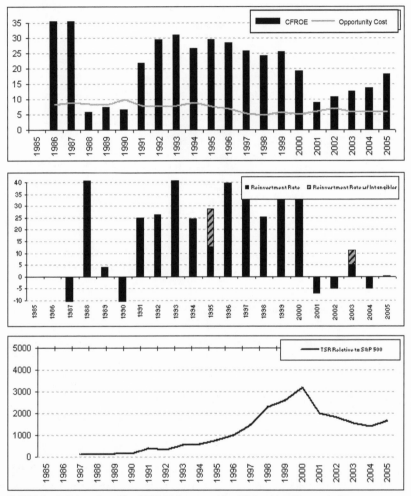

Charles Schwab has been innovative in compensating employees in line with the firm's business strategy. Unlike typical brokerage houses, Schwab based itself in San Francisco, paid employees with higher salaries, lower commissions (relative to typical Wall Street), and other aspects that truly changed the type of employees they'd attract, with 'best place to work' awards that fit the overall strategy.

From 1991 to 2000, Schwab enjoyed phenomenal CFROI returns and growth, contributing to a decade straight of rising valuations, outperforming the US market average by a whopping 30 times. While the firm was hit hard by the burst of the tech bubble in 2001, it has regained its CFROI level, but not growth.

170

Merrill Lynch (MER)

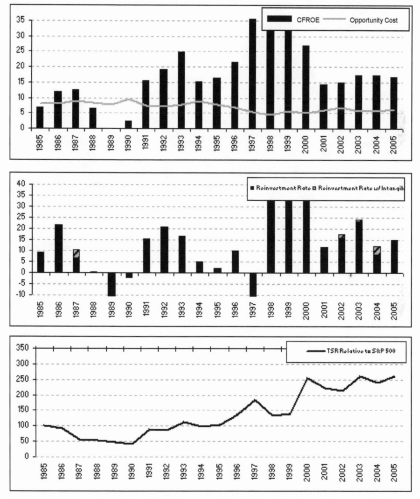

From 1991 to 2000, Merrill was far more a traditional brokerage as it had lower relative base salaries (as a percent of total compensation), but higher commissions and bonuses. With main brokerage offices in New York City along with the compensation system, attributes combined to offer a very, very different work experience than that of Schwab over the same period. Meanwhile, Merrill still was awarded 'best place to work' recognition, as was Schwab.

The firm enjoyed high CFROI levels and growth rates over the time period. This highlights the importance of aligning the *offering to employees* with the services required for executing on the particular business strategy.

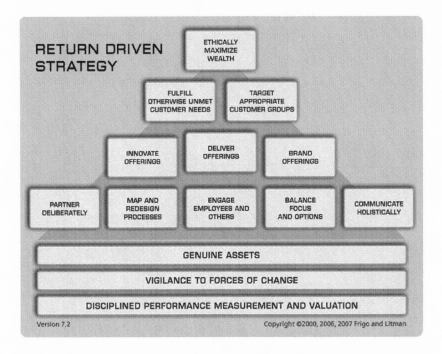

10

Tenet Ten

Balance Focus And Options

As one of the five 'Supporting Tenets,' Tenet Ten highlights how return-driven firms succeed over long periods of time by balancing focus and flexibility in planning and execution. With this, they march toward achievement of the higher tenets.

- Manage uncertainty in business planning. Not only is the future unknown, but so often is the present, as the frailty of human perception resides in everyone.

- Build flexibility into business plans, and attempt to allocate resources in ways that avoid 'points of no return' when creative planning can allow this flexibility

- Plan with questions, and create a natural bias toward questioning while building a culture that avoids having to 'prove one was right.'

- Employ Genuine Assets to build flexible plans in ways others cannot, and use options to build the potential for future Genuine Assets amidst uncertainty.

- Be vigilant to forces of change that affect the uncertainty in the environment that yields risks and opportunities, and adjust the business to prepare for potential changes by properly allocating resources in necessary real options

- Create performance measurement systems that allow for resources to be spent on maintaining flexibility in the achievement of the higher tenets

Pharma: focusing with options

The world's largest pharmaceutical companies include Pfizer, Johnson & Johnson, and Glaxo-Smith Kline. They collectively display high returns on investment that span 15 years or more, higher than average growth rates with revenues in the tens of billions, and commensurate valuation levels.

What's common about these firms? They have focused, with options. Under incredibly uncertain conditions, the firms create a drug development process that can yield phenomenal results. The drug development pipeline is one that uses options and the staging of resources to create the best platforms for creating unique need-fulfilling offerings.

Achievement through uncertainty

In order to best accomplish *any* of the tenets, uncertainty must be managed, taking advantage of opportunities and reducing risks. Often, the perception of history is revised, and so 'facts' that drive business planning always contain some level of uncertainty.

To maximize wealth, high-performance managers have a healthy respect for the uncertainty of the future and the frailty of perception. The one certain thing about any forecast is that forecasts are always wrong, but by how much? Time and again, even our assessments of our current environment need to be called into question.

Opportunities may exist and risks may lie where managers least expect them. As a steward of assets and people, successful managers balance a portfolio of activities and options in harmony with the uncertainty of perception and forecasts.

Uncertainty may or may not be a bad thing

The belief that uncertainty equals risk is simply not substantiated. Certainly, risks in a business must be controlled, managed, and mitigated. However, risk is only the downside of uncertainty. The upside of uncertainty is opportunity.

People new to the finance world will first come across the importance of risk in understanding the value of companies. They will often make a statement such as, *"Uncertainty increases risk and lowers valuations."* However, as students of finance later study in options and volatility, uncertainty can also increase valuations.

Firms exhibiting high returns – whether they be pharmaceuticals, consumer goods, or technology firms – all of them *leverage uncertainty* in order to succeed.

Some uncertainties can be controlled...
and some shouldn't be

Many managers reach a point in their career because they are great at important aspects of execution and Tenet Four. Project management is an important skill, where roles are determined, deadlines set, and processes tracked with deep attention to detail.

Certain types of uncertainty can be managed the same way. Firms can pay for insurance policies for certain identifiable risks. Controls can be put in place to better ensure worker safety. Quality tests can be done to determine that product quality meets promised levels and customer expectations.

However, the upside of uncertainty, the opportunities, cannot be so tightly managed. Ironically, very tight management is a sure-fire way of missing out on potential opportunities.

The beauty of options

Some of the highest value creators in the world are the better venture capital firms (VCs). They provide funding to very 'risky' business opportunities in hopes of the business succeeding with extremely high returns. They are experts in start-up businesses, incredibly diligent in evaluating business plans and entrepreneurial management teams. They assist ultra-high growth firms in managing through ultra-high growing pains.

With 20-30 companies or more in a VC portfolio at one time, the VC firm has fairly *no idea* which one of the investments will pay off. No investment is certain, no matter how perfect the business opportunity. Even if everything about the business is forecast to look like a perfect step-by-step representation of the Return Driven Strategy framework, still little is absolutely certain. Perceptions are regularly wrong. Forecasts are always wrong, by some amount.

So, by having 20-30 real options in owning 20-30 or more separate businesses, the VC firm both reduces its risk and increases its opportunity at the same time. As long as any one of the firm's investments is gauged to pay off by 10x or more, only 3 out of 30 ventures needs to succeed. The return on a single VC investment can be 30x or more, justifying the other failed yet similarly promising investments.

Through a portfolio of options, a business can both reduce risk and increase opportunities, as long as each option is chosen and managed well, both individually and relative to the total.

Applying options to *one* business

One giant, risky investment could be too much for a single firm. However, a recipe for longer-term success may be twenty smaller risky investments, allocated in stages with adequate but limited amounts of capital and resources at each stage.

Just as lightning strikes, firms achieve higher performance

Has anyone ever seen a straight bolt of lightning? Despite what we may have learned in school, the shortest path from point A to point B is almost never a straight line, at least not when 'shortest' is defined by least time and effort, or least resistance.

Lightning represents a high amount of electrical power, going from point A to point B – as in from the sky to the ground. Electricity seeks the path of least resistance. However, no one ever sees a straight bolt of lightning because a straight line is never the least-resistant path.

From the sky to the ground, the lightning follows a number of potential paths with different branches and forks. Some branches are dead ends and never reach the ground. The lightning never flows in a straight line because the variables that cause resistance in the air and in the weather simply make a quickly shifting and bending pattern the most efficient, just as every picture of a lightning bolt shows.

In just about anything in nature – plants, trees, migration patterns, rivers, whatever one can think of – a straight line simply does not happen naturally. It's simply not the best path. Despite the flexibility, plants still grow toward the sun, birds fly north and south seasonally, and rivers meander. The goals are still achieved, but the paths in between are flexible, bending, and shifting as the other variables demand.

It would be extremely difficult to assume that a business environment can somehow violate nature's laws in order to fabricate a straight path that appears efficient, but is anything but. Managers aim for high returns and wealth-creation, but must be flexible to change the chosen path.

There is uncertainty in all business. We cannot know ahead of time what the shortest path will be to any objective. To manage through uncertainty, managers need to plan for forks, for branches, for dead-ends. If a lightning bolt 'decided' ahead of time to go one particular branch without shifting as the elements would suggest, regardless of how much power is in the bolt, it may never reach its destination.

Flexibility can still have focus

The straight line concept is an enticing one. It makes the job of the manager much easier as targets are set for the year, and then met. However, low return businesses often exhibit an over-emphasis on rigid objective-setting that does not allow for flexibility. These firms pride them on setting targets and meeting them, even when larger more important goals are squandered. Changes in the business environment are ignored, and business activities fail to adjust as necessary.

Becoming comfortable with uncertainty can be difficult, but the higher tenets can be a powerful guide. Goals are necessary, but achieving a project deadline, or meeting earnings estimates, or hitting sales quotas are all immaterial to returns and wealth-creation if the business is unable to fulfill otherwise unmet customer needs. Meanwhile, short-term quarterly earnings estimates can be missed. Product launches can fall past their deadlines. Yet, success results if other risks are avoided and opportunities arise that allow the business to better innovate, brand, and deliver unique offerings that customers love, regardless of what happens this quarter.

The best laid plans...

Many successful venture capital firms have stated something similar to the following,

> *"I'd rather have an A-team with a B-plan than a B-team with an A-plan."*

Every successful venture capital firm and experienced leader knows that there is only one certainty about a business plan – nothing predicted is certain. Down the road, things will go differently from what has been planned, no matter how much research has gone into the planning.

As the business is being built, new information is learned about customers, customer segments, shifting technologies, or a myriad of other potential events. An A-team manager is a flexible one, who can adjust for those changes in the business plan, while still being highly motivated and focused on the goal of wealth-creation. Options-thinking requires flexibility.

Flexibility to allow for 'failures'

Flexibility means planning options into each business path that allow for the firm to be more nimble and agile. It also allows the firm to be set up for take advantage of unexpected opportunities.

In resource allocation, managers need to be prepared to give up certain 'causes' when enough signposts tell the firm to go a different way. 'Sunk costs' describe previous investments of time and resources into a particular project. Managers can have an emotional attachment to sunk costs. Along with a need to be proven right, these attachments can cause a manager to throw even more bad investments toward an already bad business.

Failure needs to be seen as an acceptable part of every business if it wants to succeed in the long-term. However, failures need to occur at the right levels and at the right times, relative to the rest of the business.

Flexibility implies preparation for and expectation that certain projects will not work, certain offerings will not sell, and certain business units will need to be divested. High-performing leaders know that failed projects, offerings, or business units don't necessarily imply that it was a mistake to launch those initiatives. If risks are taken at the right levels and with the right level of monitoring, one would expect every successful company to be littered with small tiny failures, on the road to giant successes.

Successful management teams evaluate performance at a higher portfolio level of project success rates in the achievement of the higher tenets, and not at an individual initiative level.

Balancing exploration with execution

A key to leveraging options strategy is in balancing the amount of resources that go to new initiatives with resources toward existing ones. Successful firms should try to not have all of its initiatives focused on innovation or all focused on branding. A balance is needed between initiatives that support the three competencies, innovation, branding, and execution.

The amount of resources should be balanced based on the ability of the mix of activities to create a business that can fulfill otherwise unmet customer needs. With each option or initiative, successful managers generally look to start small, but ramp up fast as the situation suggests. Tenet Two slightly overrides Tenet Three as a firm can be patient with dominating the market, but be urgent about determining ways to fulfill unmet need.

Concluding notes on Tenet Ten

"At birth all people are soft and yielding.
At death they are hard and stiff.
All green plants are tender and yielding.
At death they are brittle and dry.
When hard and rigid,
We consort with death.
When soft and flexible,
We affirm greater life."
(From the Tao Te Ching)

The natural economic collapse of totalitarian societies ranging from feudalism to the supposedly communist countries of the 20th Century stemmed in part from an inability of a government regime to control all the factors necessary to make the economy work. In essence, the most successful economies succeed by being out-of-control in terms of central management, and yet thrive through flexibility.

It would be difficult to find a more honorable statement about Return Driven Strategy than to say its research and findings are consistent with the thoughts of the late, great economist, Milton Friedman.

Friedman expressed the virtues of the free market system, with its flexibility in resource allocation and options-thinking. He raised obvious examples of the economies with strict command-and-control structures that fall behind those with flexibility.

When companies are allowed to go bankrupt and new businesses are allowed to thrive organically, everyone prevails. In the most successful economies, entire industries die regularly while new ones sprout up.

When once was a dominant agricultural society, now may be technology. Where once were horse-drawn buggies, now there may be communications highways. If successful countries thrive on uncertainty, so must companies that want to be successful. A firm that only controls risks, but does not leverage opportunities through flexibility and portfolios of options, cannot achieve highest levels of returns.

Key Diagnostics for Tenet Ten

Does the business have a way of engaging employees for long-term initiatives that may not pay off in the near-term but are central to long-term success?

Does the business approach new initiatives with staging capabilities that build-in real options and flexibility for potential uncertainties?

Does the business examine its various offerings and/or businesses as a portfolio, with a layer of planning that examines all of its offerings?

Does the business seek to harness serendipity, appropriately balancing exploration activities with execution activities necessary to achieve its higher tenets both for near-term and long-term success?

Are all options and portfolio strategies and activities performed consistently and within the parameters of the higher tenets?

Does the business use Genuine Assets to better assure achievement of this tenet? Is a process in place for building these Genuine Assets?

Is management continually on the watch for and aware of significant forces of change that could limit the firm's ability to execute on this tenet in the future?

Are the right metrics in place and reviewed regularly to help management monitor and communicate the business's ability to execute on this tenet?

Pfizer (PFE)

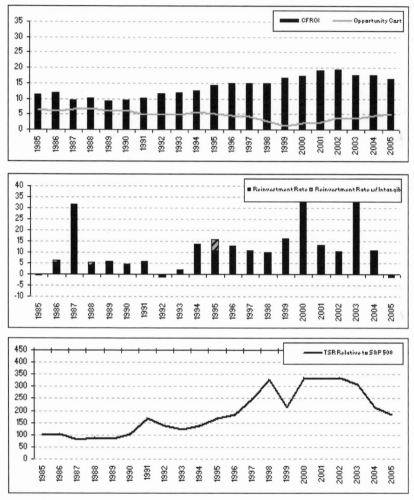

As the largest pharmaceutical company in the world, Pfizer has had to master the tenet of balancing focus with options. If the firm over-relies on near-term profits and focuses on marketing its current blockbuster drugs, long-term returns could suffer. And so, it has what could be called the largest research and development organization of all pharmaceuticals.

Yet, if the firm over-invests in high-potential drugs that may not be ready for years, and under-invests in the marketing and distribution of drugs coming out sooner, value will still not be maximized. By balancing today's focus with the real options for tomorrow, PFE has been a phenomenal performer.

183

Sanofi-Aventis (SASY)

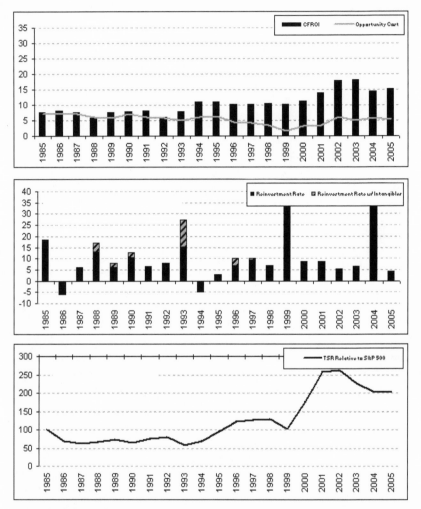

Based in France, Sanofi-Aventis is one of the five largest pharma companies in the world. In seven major therapeutic areas, the firm balances focus and options with a drug pipeline they call "the life cycle of a drug from research to patients." Of every 10,000 compounds, only one will become a medicinal product. The cycle can take fifteen years on average. Resources must be carefully managed over each stage of a potential drug's development or all resources can be squandered. If successful, the firm can create an offering that can fulfill the need of "the constant improvement of human health."

Glaxosmithkline PLC (GSK)

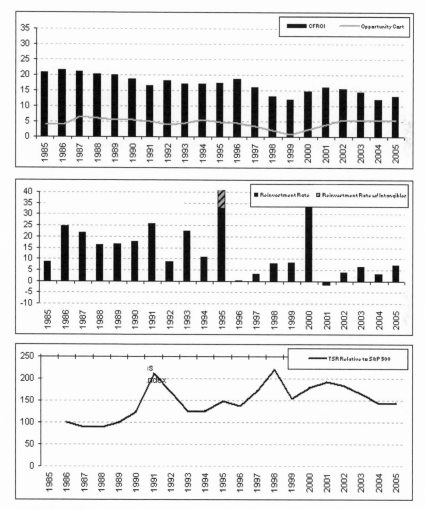

Based in Britain, Glaxosmithkline's CFROI levels have never fallen below 10%. High reinvestment rates from 1985 to 1991 delivered extraordinary stock performance. Expensive acquisitions and much lower organic growth rates from 1996 to 2005 have forced the stock markets to reduce their valuations of the firm, but it still cumulatively outperforms the major London stock market index from levels 20 years earlier.

As common with firms achieving high performance, a mission statement focuses on customer needs, "...enabling people to do more, feel better, and live longer." Developing offerings for this need, the firm posted high CFROI returns.

185

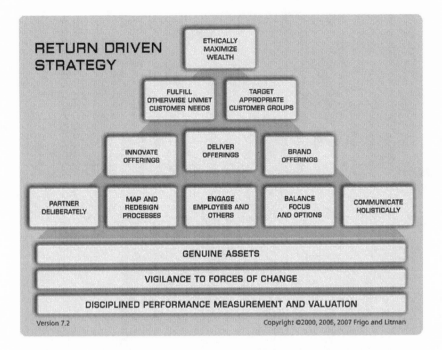

11

Tenet Eleven

Communicate Holistically

Tenet Eleven is one of the five 'Supporting Tenets.' High performance comes from understanding the integral role of communications throughout the entire business, including business planning.

- Utilize a wide range of communications creatively, recognizing each type's merits and purpose

- Design communications with the specific purpose of achieving the higher tenets, noting how every communication has the potential to impact all aspects of the business, not just the ones intended

- Assume that no communication can be kept completely secret, and eventually anything worth hearing about probably will be heard

- Develop and deliver offerings to not only communicate the attributes of the offering, but also to be part and parcel of the offering itself in the mind of the customer

- Employ Genuine Assets that allow the firm to develop and create communications in ways other firms cannot replicate in achievement of the higher tenets.

- Be vigilant to forces of change that affect the types of communications available and the interpretations of them.

- Create performance measures that allow communications to be managed and their impact well-understood consistently with the whole system of tenets

Communicating for the whole

No verbal or nonverbal communication can be made in one part of a business without potentially impacting every other part. High-return firms create communication strategies that take all of the tenets into consideration. Holistic communications are made with the whole of the business in mind.

A communications program becomes incredibly valuable when it balances all of the objectives of the firm as set forth by the higher tenets. Given that every action and even non-action of a firm is implicitly a form of communication, the far-ranging implications of this tenet on all other tenets becomes apparent.

Impacting people, impacting thought

Tenet Eleven is the fifth of five Supporting Tenets, anchoring the right corner of the pyramid. Its position as number eleven does not suggest its unimportance to a business. On the contrary, it is of utmost importance in a business's ability to succeed.

The adage 'think before you speak' can be applied to this tenet. When *planning* a business, the communication strategy of high return firms always follows the other tenets. How the firm communicates, what it communicates, when and why, should all be determined by the firm's plans to ethically maximize wealth as it has been defined.

Communications impact thoughts. The thoughts of the customers, employees, vendors, partners, and the public at large will determine the success or failure of a business. Are the constituents' thoughts about the business good ones or bad ones?

Thought Smith

John Sviokla is vice-chairman of Diamond Management and Technology Consultants, one of the most innovative firms in its industry since its inception. Previously, Sviokla was a professor at Harvard Business School where he coined the term 'marketspace.' He created the term to describe the fall of physical boundaries when targeting customers in the digital age – from market 'place' to marketspace. Changing environments may require new terms to communicate what one is thinking – or would like others to consider.

Sviokla has personally worked with hundreds of companies in redefining and recrafting their business strategies. In one instance, he was working with a management team in a final iteration of the executive summary before meeting with investors. To help the team focus, Sviokla said the following on the importance of these iterations,

> *"People will rewrite their messages and often call it word-smithing, but we need to realize that we're doing much more than that. It's really* 'thought-smithing.' *The exact words we choose to use can dramatically change how people think about the message."*

The phrase 'arguing semantics' is sometimes used to discount the importance of specific word choices during debates. However, the exact words used can change the meaning of the discussion. Semantics may deserve argument. John provides a strong message about the role and application of communications in business planning.

Communicating with what purpose?

Whether targeting customers, employees, or investors, the purpose of the communication is more effective when the focus is on a desired action: to get the customer to buy; to encourage the employee to stay longer, to convince the investor to not sell the stock. Whatever it is, there is some end purpose which should be considered as the communication method, style, tone, etc., are chosen.

The current culture of *everything-can-be-emailed* seems to have led to a loss in creativity of communications. It ignores a long menu of choices in communications, often missing the right one for the right task at hand.

> *"What is the best reasonable outcome from this particular communication?"*

For examples, return-driven leaders intuitively consider whether breakfast, lunch, or dinner would be the appropriate timing for a particular discussion. Given the location, the time of day, and the level of stress, people actually *think differently.* So, if the purpose of communication is to impact thought, should not other thought-impacting variables be considered?

The importance of best planning the right communication *to impact thought* cannot be understated. A small list of communications would include:

> *Email, personal phone calls, blast voicemails, face-to-face discussions at a meal or over coffee or drinks, word of mouth, bills and invoices, press releases, press conferences, articles, books, websites...*

Choosing the right communication can make all the difference between business success and failure. In fact, everything the firm does or does not do that a person thinks about is explicitly or implicitly impacting their thought, and need be considered as a communication.

To fulfill unmet needs, one needs to discover them

In studying the great salespeople of the world, whether in real estate, business services, products, or concepts, one finds they are not the ones with the best presentations.

Communication is a two-way street. Great salespeople are the ones *with the best questions.* They don't impress a client by showing off how smart they are. They impress the client by asking insightful questions that determine the customer's specific, compelling, unique need.

Great salespeople also repeat the customer's answer back to them in order to determine that they have heard the answer correctly and also potentially gather more insight into the customer's need. This process of listening, asking questions, and then listening more intently is sometimes referred to as *active listening*. Armed with unique information about the customer, it's much easier to provide an offering that fulfills their most compelling needs uniquely.

Through surveys, focus groups, feedback forms, product tests, and myriads of other methods, they *listen and watch for* the needs of customers. Colgate-Palmolive, with some of the most consistently high returns of any industry, collects information from millions upon millions of customer touch-points in order to gather information to better plan its business initiatives.

Undoubtedly, any great menu of types of communications would begin with methods for getting the customers, employees, and other business partners to communicate *their thoughts* to the firm.

The communication is part of the offering

Customers perceive them to have scarcity of resources and time. An effective communication strategy does many things:

- Gathers information about the customer's needs for innovating the offering

- Brands the offering, connecting the offering to their explicitly understood personal need

- Provides information for the delivery and utilization of the offering

- Allows for feedback during and after use of the offering

- Induces happy customers to tell others who have similar need and encourages not-so-happy customers to direct their issues to the firm

Given the importance and inseparability of each of these important purposes of communications, one must see the communication as part and parcel of the offering itself.

Two-way streets go in all directions

In the earlier days of Yahoo, it had achieved remarkable status as one of the most viewed websites. As a portal, its reach into the eyes and minds of Internet surfers was phenomenal. However, it was unclear as to how Yahoo would generate revenue outside of advertising. Investors were clamoring for more information as to how the firm could *monetize* the great amount of attention it was receiving.

The firm built one of the most successful partnerships with small and large businesses that wanted to sell products over the web, called Yahoo Store. Businesses eager to sell their wares through Yahoo's online network and search engine paid a monthly fee and shared revenue per item sold. The strategy was working very well, with businesses of all kinds and sizes.

In April of 2001, on an investor relations conference call, Yahoo sought to inform investors of how promising their revenues could be. It specifically called out one area of growth, Yahoo online stores that were allowing vendors to sell 'adult goods and novelties.'

For years, the Internet had shown itself to be incredibly profitable in this industry, allowing customer discretion in purchase. Yahoo was simply stating that it had tapped into this high-growth, high-profit market.

Yahoo was already part of the fabric of everyday life, and more than just investors were listening to that conference call.

Public backlash over Yahoo being seen as a purveyor of adult items was so severe that the company was actually forced to shut down many of these businesses' online presence on Yahoo. Yahoo had to go far in appeasing the groups squaring off against Yahoo's 'unethical conduct.' The company had to even shut down online stores that had been selling products regularly in shopping malls, such as joke or novelty items. Far from simply red-light-district wares, general revenue sources were being shut down.

The investor relations call not only failed to induce investors to raise the perceived valuation of the firm, but also caused them to notice real reductions in cash flows, and undoubtedly negative valuation impact. Earlier in Yahoo's life cycle, such a communication could have resulted in far higher valuations. But, higher tenets remain umbrella tenets to all the activities that fall below them. As Yahoo's presence grew among the general public, so too did the ethical standards upon which it is held. Tenet One governs.

The pen can be mightier than the sword

In the digital age, anything worth noticing will often be noticed. Regardless of how confidential, how private, or how well-encrypted, 'leaks' occur in every organization, every day.

- Personal, confidential emails have been forwarded to such a degree that people have been fired over comments made in private to others about personal exploits

- Internal company memos have been published with regularity in newspapers, websites, and in court cases. Some of these have led to successful multi-billion dollar lawsuits

- People have innocently hit 'reply to all' keys about sensitive employee information (this happens so often and to so many that it's a wonder it hasn't obstructed the use of "reply-to-all" emails in the first place)

- Detailed accounts of interactions and discussions have surfaced when 'everyone agreed and signed to confidentiality'

- Memos that show that giant consumer product firms sold products that they were aware were unhealthy, while the firms advertised otherwise

- Password-protected spreadsheets complete with salary, bonus, and promotion information of *entire firms* have been unlocked and widely distributed, sometimes months before people have even received their bonus or promotion

All the attorneys, internet security consultants, and personal pledges in the world cannot solve the dilemma of 'word getting out.' Which leads to one of the core elements of Tenet Eleven:

> *Assume that everything you say or type will*
> *eventually be heard and read by everyone.*

Each tenet falls under an overriding umbrella of the highest tenet, ethically maximizing wealth. Ethics are defined by the communities in which a firm operates. Yahoo had also reached the level of impact on society that is enjoyed by few other firms, such as Wal-Mart, Microsoft, and McDonald's. For firms of their span and scope, society dictates a higher standard of ethics than it does for smaller businesses – or at least is far more vocal and active about its standards with these super-size firms than with others.

At some level of the integration of a firm's offerings with society, society *sees the firm almost as their own.* This can affect the business dramatically. So, had Yahoo been a smaller player on the Internet, or had been involved more with business to business offerings, it might not have received the backlash from its conference call that it did.

> *Act in accordance with other tenets, particularly*
> *Tenet One, Ethically Maximize Wealth*

Who is everyone? Constituents of the firm include investors/owners, other managers, employees, business partners, customers, the general public, the potential public if new markets are entered, the government, and certainly, competition.

With every communication, expect a potential impact from all constituents, not simply the ones being spoken to, *and communicate accordingly.*

No communication can be made to one constituent of the firm without being available to another. And every communication needs to fall within the parameters of the higher tenets. This is not always easy.

The truth will be revealed

Recent developments in voice recognition technology and analysis have led to an ability to detect emotion, cognitive functions, and "intent to deceive" based on the spoken word. The technology appears to work over-the-phone and through conference calls. Security and law enforcement applications are a natural market for this technology. Far beyond that, other commercial applications are springing up.

Some investors have begun utilizing these technologies when listening to management conference calls. Investment decisions will include the impact of voice analysis that suggests levels of stress, confusion, and "creativity" on these calls. The investors focus on the potential to detect when management may overly hype, or sandbag, earnings guidance and sales forecasts.

Insurance companies are using these technologies when examining people's insurance claims. The technology is used to identify claims of higher risk to assign to insurance investigators. One insurance firm stated that it would never attempt to deny a claim based on deception technology results. Instead, it allocates its investigative resources toward higher risk claims as the technology identifies. The firm believes this process has reduced their claims expense by 25% since inception.

Marketing firms have begun adding this capability to focus groups and customer interviews. How often does a person respond with the answer they think the interviewer wants to hear as opposed to what is truly felt?

The digital age and the insights of Tenet Eleven call on the manager to simply speak the truth – or possibly to not speak at all...

Saying nothing says something

Return-driven firms expect there to be important communications that impact constituents beyond those explicitly stated: non-responses to customers, nonverbal actions of the firm, experiences with competing offerings, the store, site, or other location or any touch-point in which the person purchases or interacts with the business.

Some of these touch points can be controlled and leveraged, some can't be. To be safe, one might consider everything to be a potential communication. What is the best solution? If the firm follows the tenets as outlined in Return Driven Strategy, every activity of the firm becomes a potential communication that supports the strategy of the organization.

Concluding notes on Tenet Eleven

In discussions of communications strategy, the question can be raised, 'is the pen mightier than the sword?' What is the power of communications when viewed in light of all of the tenets? The pen may or may not be mightier than the sword, but no doubt the pen and sword together are a powerful combination for creating wealth.

People are inundated with communications of many kinds. The more the communications of a firm are integrated with the entire framework of Return Driven Strategy, the more likely those communications will not fall on deaf ears. This is what's implied by the term, 'holistic.'

When communications are viewed strategically, managers do not limit their thinking to outbound messages, but understand a means for interacting with the constituents of the firm in the true sense of a community. In and of itself that is one of the basic needs of humanity, as outlined by Abraham Maslow.

The lasting messages, from the explicit or implied communications around an offering, are inseparable from the offering in the mind of the customer. Better communications strategies not only succeed in a task of exchanging information, but also in positively impacting people's hearts, minds, and lives.

Key Diagnostics for Tenet Eleven

Are all communications strategies made consistently and within the parameters of all of the other Eleven Tenets, particularly Tenet One?

Specifically, do communications support the branding, innovating, and operations plans?

Are communication strategies seen as two-way streets, with active listening and information collection seen as being just as important as outbound communications?

Are the right types of communications utilized to help re-strategize and execute on the Eleven Tenets based on information received?

Are all communications made with the notion: "Assume that everyone everywhere can and will eventually hear or read everything you say or type?"

Does the business use Genuine Assets to better assure achievement of this tenet? Is a process in place for building these Genuine Assets?

Is management continually on the watch for and aware of significant forces of change that could limit the firm's ability to execute on this tenet in the future?

Are the right metrics in place and reviewed regularly to help management monitor and communicate the business's ability to execute on this tenet?

Paychex Inc. (PAYX)

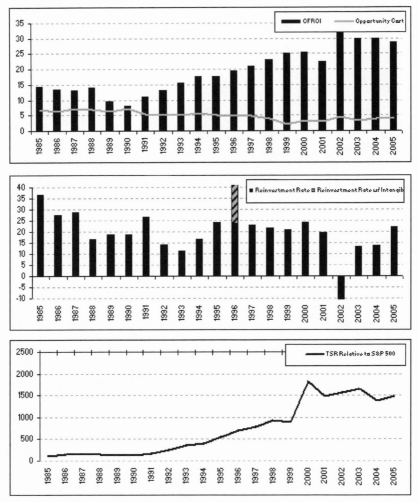

Paychex is a national provider of payroll and related outsourcing solutions for businesses. The meteoric rise in CFROI returns since 1990, coupled with high growth rates, has led to performance 15 times the US market.

One vehicle the firm has used to communicate with small and medium-sized businesses is local accounting (CPA) firms that service the targeted customer groups. Because payroll and benefits systems can be extremely complex, a CPA cannot only explain the difficult financial issues, but also send a message of confidence with the CPA's implicit and explicit endorsement. This is one example of how Paychex's communications strategy supported its overall strategy via the higher tenets.

Yahoo (YHOO)

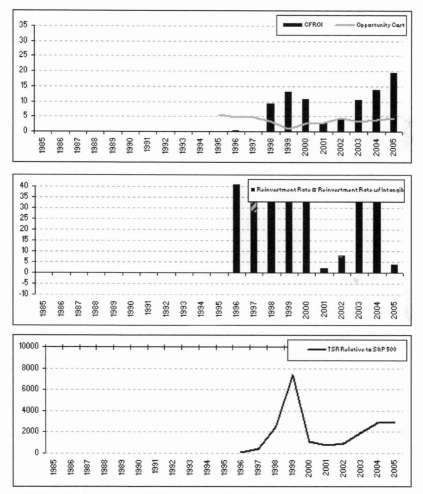

During Yahoo's two worst years after the burst of the tech bubble, 2000 and 2001, the company struggled to achieve CFROI levels at the cost of capital. The firm's communications strategy also exhibited struggle.

On a conference call with shareholders in April 2001, Yahoo heralded its success in generating revenues from sales of vendors' adult-themed goods. However, any communication is a communication available to all. Instead of boosting valuation, there was backlash from family-oriented groups who considered those revenues unethical. Yahoo was forced to divest itself of the partnerships that generated these revenues, further hurting valuations at the time. All activities fall under Tenet One. Since then, CFROI levels and growth have recovered impressively, as valuation changes reflect.

Part Five

The Foundations

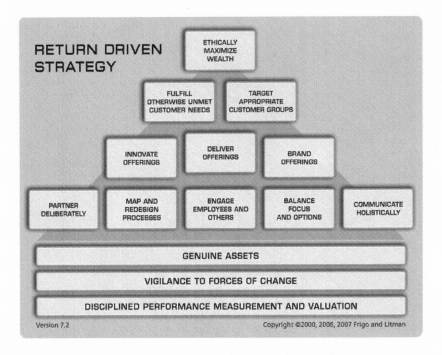

12

The Foundations

Genuine Assets

While the Eleven Tenets are the 'verbs' of strategy, the Genuine Assets are the 'nouns.' Genuine Assets are the building blocks for creating walls to protect against competition.

Any activity can be copied by competitors as soon as they see high returns or the potential for them. That leads to price competition and lower cash flow returns. However, unique, Genuine Assets, when leveraged appropriately, can be used to create offerings in ways no one else can, sustaining returns for decades or more and creating a foundation for unparalleled growth.

Building blocks of long-term competitive advantage

Genuine Assets can be examined tenet by tenet as means for resisting the natural fade in performance that firms experience from competition. Unique assets make for unique activities and are thereby genuine in nature and not able to be copied by competitors. However, uniqueness in and of itself is not inherently valuable.

Each example of a Genuine Asset focuses on the tenets. The formula always requires the *noun* and the *verb*. No asset is valuable if it does not have the potential to generate future returns. Whether or not it has been explicitly stated, every high-return example shown in each of the eleven tenets has a set of Genuine Assets that fortify its returns.

For explanation purposes, the pyramid describes eleven distinct concepts. It's difficult to discuss one tenet without at least hinting at its effect on the others. So, in practice, the tenets interact and overlap with each other. Successful firms' activities are aligned toward the top of the pyramid. Genuine Assets should not simply be leveraged in one tenet, but should be used to achieve all of the tenets, and ultimately wealth-creation.

The Microsoft OS

Microsoft created a Genuine Asset with its Windows OS (operating system). This served as a platform for competitive advantage for many different offerings. In and of itself, it was a unique for fulfilling otherwise unmet needs, as evidenced by the incredible market domination of Windows on computers throughout the world.

The operating system was also a Genuine Asset for achieving the tenets in many other ways. With patents over its system, the firm was uniquely able to produce software and license other developers. In turn, more unique offerings were created. Many of Microsoft's products were not first movers. But, the Genuine Asset of the operating system made it easy to target customer needs in ways no one else could.

Microsoft utilized the unique, non-copiable operating system and its large user base to push through what many thought were applications inferior in capability, except one very important trait. The programs could 'talk' to each other relatively easily, and many commands such as 'cut-and-paste' were identical key strokes across the systems.

Word soon over took WordPerfect in word processing software. Excel overtook the spreadsheet market from Lotus 123. PowerPoint had all but completely replaced other previously used graphic presentation applications. The Access database software became dominant in its category. In each of these areas, the *first mover lost.* The Genuine Assets define who has the potential to create a monopoly in otherwise equal competitions. Functional product attributes as businesses perceive them are not necessarily the path to wealth-creation, no matter how innovative.

Customers were willing to forego the bleeding edge functionality of WordPerfect, Lotus 123, and other programs in exchange for more basic functionality that could be successfully used together. At the time, the ability to more easily cut-and-paste from Word to Excel was more valuable than the most advanced word processing and spreadsheet features that Microsoft's products didn't yet have.

Development, management, and leveraging of Genuine Assets have formed the foundation of Microsoft's success. Its history of cash flows is one the best ever seen. Through the unique and legally non-copiable operating system, the company succeeded in better fulfilling the otherwise unmet needs of more and more targeted customer groups.

GE's 'Deep Bench'

One of GE's many Genuine Assets is a deep bench of high-performance managers who are regularly recruited out of GE and into key management positions at other companies around the world. In fact, more CEOs of large companies are alumni of GE than of any other company. Meanwhile, GE enjoys a large base of up-and-coming managers throughout its ranks.

Many new graduates will pass up job offers of higher immediate compensation in exchange for 'getting into GE' in order to be ingrained in the GE philosophy. The company has been able to sustain returns and competitive advantages in its business lines for more than two decades.

This Genuine Asset allows the firm to recruit and engage top employees in ways extremely difficult to match by most other companies. As they execute and further develop the firm's Six Sigma methodology, the company executes on business strategies as a model for Tenet Four (as discussed in Chapter Four).

Their focus on the right measures and metrics for wealth-creation, such as growth and return on invested capital, has created a company whose entire culture strives toward the high returns the company exhibits. An operations management framework such as Six Sigma that GE developed can be copied by others, but years of being trained and ingrained in a culture driven toward returns and wealth-creation is not easily replicated.

Harley Owners Group (HOG)

The Harley Owners Group is unique. Many companies wish they had such an avid, engaged customer base. The Genuine Asset lies in the way Harley-Davidson has utilized this singular phenomenon to better identify and understand the otherwise unmet needs of Harley customers. HOG has contributed to branding the firm's products and providing information for innovations that has not been paralleled in the automotive industry. So different is the business model, that many wouldn't call Harley an automotive firm.

HOG was formed in 1983 to encourage Harley owners to become more actively involved in the sport of motorcycling. In 2004, HOG worldwide membership reached 900,000 in comparison with competitors such as Honda's Gold Wing Road Riders Association which had less than a tenth that number.

HOG has grown to well over a million members. Many HOG members are employees along with the unique employee engagement that can thereby be created. It gives Harley-Davidson the ability to offer its customers a best-practice model for communicating holistically. In many ways, purchasing a Harley and gaining entry into HOG is part and parcel of the unique offering itself.

Wal-Mart's ERP System

Enterprise Resource Planning systems help to connect the disparate functions of a firm and better manage large corporations. Wal-Mart's system is second-to-none. It allows the firm to have a firm handle on exactly what customers are buying and when. With a unique asset such as this, Wal-Mart has been able to garner more than 10% of all US retail purchases through its stores.

After the terrorist strike on the US on 9/11, Wal-Mart was one of the first to stock its shelves with an abundance of American flags. After natural disasters, the company is often first to have ample supplies needed by the people struck by the disaster. Time and again, the ERP system has given Wal-Mart a knowledge base and an operational agility that possibly no other retailer enjoys.

Dominating its targeted customer groups far beyond other retailers, the company has accomplished this so efficiently that even with the lowest prices, it sustains the highest long-term track record of returns of any retailer. Others simply have not been able to develop such a strong ERP system for managing the incredible logistics behind a company that's bigger than many countries. This singularity creates a foundation for the firm to dominate considerably large customer groups, fulfill their needs uniquely, and thereby generate incredible returns and wealth.

DBS: The Danaher Business System

Danaher remains to be the company that no one hears of despite its incredible prowess. Phenomenal returns and growth rates over decades has generated a market valuation in excess of $22 billion dollars. The firm has been singular in its ability to continually buy up smaller, poorly-managed firms, and then improve them remarkably with DBS.

The Danaher Business System incorporates a number of processes and business improvement systems with a customer-oriented philosophy. This system has helped the company to generate returns on acquisitions that are the envy of any high growth firm. The core values of DBS can be read almost as a checklist for Return Driven Strategy.

With this system, the firm can execute on its strategies in ways few other firms have been able to. The acquisitions, injected with DBS, push the partnering tenet to wealth-creating heights. The returns and wealth-creation of the firm reflect this acumen.

Concluding notes on Genuine Assets

Activities can be copied. High-return activities will be copied more quickly. The Nobel Laureate George Stigler noted how, over time, high-return firms attract attention from new entrants. Competitive advantages of firms and industries are diminished and returns eventually fade to corporate averages.

However, in a study of tens of thousands of firms, a relative few show an ability to drive cash flow returns upward over time, fighting the natural competitive fade that Stigler describes. These high-performance firms fortify their activities with Genuine Assets that prevent others from doing the same.

DRIVEN

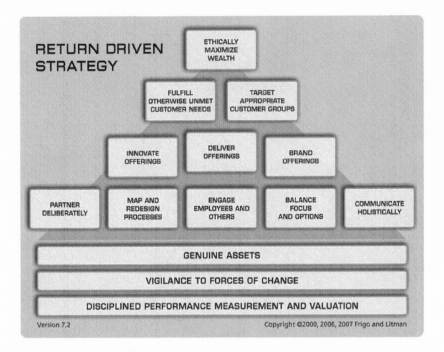

13

The Foundations

Vigilance to Forces of Change

'Delta' is the fourth letter in the Greek alphabet and is the symbol for 'change.' The backdrop of the pyramid of tenets is a triangle, for this particular reason. It is the second of three foundations that return-driven firms consider with every tenet and in the overall strategy to drive high returns and wealth-creation.

Business environments are incredibly dynamic. High-performance firms take advantage of opportunities and avoid threats in each of the tenets that are brought about by changes. Historically, forces of change can be viewed through three key lenses.

Scientific and Technological Breakthroughs

Forces of change can be seen in scientific and technological break-throughs such as the invention of the printing press. The advent of readily copiable and thereby available newspapers and books changed the very fabric of society. New businesses cropped up as the technology took hold. New services were required.

Other examples include railroads and automobiles. More recent examples include the personal computer, the Internet, wireless networks, and broadband connectivity. As each of these technologies arises, a ripple effect occurs through each of the tenets. New ways of understanding customer need takes shape, along with new ways of fulfilling them. New customer groups become targetable, with new ways of dominating them. As this happened, previously successful business models begin to fail, just as the horse-drawn carriage became obsolete.

Population and demographic shifts

Other sources of change can be viewed through shifting demographics. As rural areas have become urbanized, new modes of transportation are required, and the culture of the population changes.

Other examples include an increased need for convenience as people complain of having less and less time in the day. The Age Wave describes population levels across age groups and its effects have been well-researched by author Ken Dychtwald. Population "waves" can alter entire economic landscapes.

Harley-Davidson targeted the baby boomers, one of the peak population groups in the age wave. As this group had more wealth and more leisure time to enjoy the motorcycle, one can see similar high-growth patterns in Harley's cash flows.

Statutory and regulatory change

Financial services deregulation allowed for the very existence of firms like Charles Schwab and has impacted its growth opportunities over the years. Other actions of the government such as airline deregulation, utilities deregulation, and anti-trust acts can mean life or death for a particular business strategy.

Vigilance

Forces of change don't necessarily mean problems if the business is vigilant and adjusts strategies accordingly. As any potentially disruptive change is in sight, high-performance managers change the targeted customer groups, change their offerings, adjust how they hire employees, and every other aspect of the pursuit of the Eleven Tenets.

Management teams that cling to outmoded strategies and techniques are doomed. In each of these cases, there is a distinct human characteristic, a flaw in judgment, an inability to let go of the past, despite signs telling the manager to do so.

'If change is happening on the outside faster than on the in-side, the end is in sight.' – Jack Welch, former CEO of GE

Control what you can. Understand what you can't control

Forces of Change can rock the business from all directions. Some forces of change are slow and predictable; some are sudden and unexpected. Others appear to be random.

The fact is that Forces of Change drive the risks and opportunities of all businesses. How well management understands and manages these risks and opportunities will determine the firm's success or failure.

Strategy is dynamic, not static

There is a common belief that 'strategy' happens at management off-sites or management retreats. The effectiveness of strategy is summarized in this quote from a manager:

"Who is out there telling people that a day-long management retreat has any lasting value? I'd rather keep working and get something valuable done."

In one example, a firm's main source of costs came from fuel. When asked why returns were so low, the firm exclaimed, *"We didn't expect oil prices to be so high."* Meanwhile, other firms in the industry were hedging oil prices, and were able to maintain more stable pricing of their offerings and more stable returns.

Successful strategic planning is not an event, it is a continual process. Low return businesses are repeatedly accompanied with a blame-mentality on external elements. The term 'blindsided' is used.

Force of Change: The 'Age Wave'

Shifting demographics and the 'Age Wave' impact every company in one way or another. The baby boom generation represents a very large group of customers. As this group ages, there will be a shift in the size and growth patterns of customer groups and levels of particular need along with it. Every tenet in the Return Driven Strategy framework must be examined in terms of this Force of Change.

For Tenet One (Ethically Maximize Wealth), a much older electorate might lead to changes in regulations. Changing regulations might affect allowed profitability levels in certain industries through price regulations and political pressure.

For Tenet Two (Fulfill Otherwise Unmet Customer Needs), an older population may seek more specialized, more customized housing and living choices.

For Tenet Three (Target Appropriate Customer Groups), some businesses serving the 70+ age group could naturally experience 20% growth rates.

Throughout the case studies in each tenet explanation in *Driven,* Forces of Change are mentioned that firms have either capitalized on or fallen victim to.

Questions to ask

Successful managers ask the following types of questions relating to this force of change:

- How will the Age Wave change the otherwise unmet needs our company fulfills?

- How will the Age Wave affect the size and growth patterns of our customer groups?

- Does the organization have the process and capabilities to monitor how the Age Wave will affect its business?

Forces of Change – Specific Events

At times, a specific event can dramatically force the firm to shift its activities. In an instant, the importance of ongoing strategic planning and adjustment becomes paramount. Johnson & Johnson has demonstrated the flexibility to Forces of Change in its response to immediate events that require action. Decades of consistently high-return performance have made it a model for understanding this foundation.

This company combines focused business-continuity planning with high ethical standards and good communication. In 2003, when Johnson & Johnson learned that its anemia drug Procrit had been counterfeited, it quickly rolled out a well-developed crisis plan and worked with customers to identify suspect product. JNJ set a rapid timeframe in which legitimate product would be tested, certified, repackaged, and shipped to customers.

J&J had a plan for execution for these types of events and the communication and culture which led management and employees to a swift resolution of the situation. The Johnson & Johnson Procrit case is consistent with the way J&J has confronted a series of business crises, from the Tylenol tampering in 1982, to Zomax, a pain medicine withdrawn from the market in 1983 after patients died from using it, to the counterfeit versions of Procrit in 2003.

In each situation, J&J executives credit the company's culture and Credo with guiding their decision making and having a disciplined execution process for getting things done. No individual event can be predicted perfectly, but the importance of expecting the events and building strategies around them has been important to the firm's success.

Vigilance makes the difference

In March 2000, what initially appeared to be a minor disruption for Nokia and Ericsson turned out to be a critical event for both companies. A lighting bolt struck a semiconductor plant that made chips for both telecom equipment makers.

Both firms received phone calls notifying them of a fire that had ruined key components that were bound for each firm. Managers at Nokia noticed a glitch in the flow of chips even before Philips told them there was a real problem. They estimated that potential impact of the disruption in the supply of chips could translate into an inability to produce four million handsets, representing 5% of the company's sales. The firm quickly worked with the supplier to re-source necessary components.

When asked about how the issue was brought to the attention of the right people at Nokia, one manager said:

> *"We encourage bad news to travel fast'...'We don't want to hide problems."*

Nokia demonstrated good strategic communication, engagement of employees, and partnering strategy. The firm demonstrated knowledge and insight on how to adjust its activities accordingly. Nokia has demonstrated one of the most impressive cash flow return histories of any company.

In contrast, Ericsson responded slowly and did not have alternative sourcing options. By the time management realized the extent of the problem, they had nowhere else to turn for several key parts. One manager at Ericsson said,

> *'We did not have a Plan B.'*

This was a major factor in Ericsson's outright exit of the phone headset production market in 2001. *(Key excerpts from 'Trial by Fire: A Blaze in Albuquerque Sets Off Major Crisis For Cell-Phone Giants' Wall Street Journal, January 29, 2001.)*

Concluding notes on Forces of Change

Benjamin Franklin was quoted as saying, "Drive thy business, or thy business will drive thee." How can a leader successfully drive the returns of the organization if the leader cannot see the road ahead?

Whether by specific events or longer term trends, business environments change, often dramatically, that require the business to adjust as well. Over time, high return businesses have proven an ability to adjust as necessary, throughout every tenet.

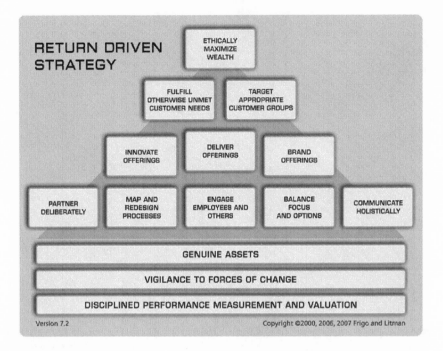

14

The Foundations

Disciplined Performance Measurement and Valuation

The Return Driven Strategy framework is founded on a comprehensive understanding of the connection between strategy, execution, performance, and valuation.

Rigorous performance measurement is necessary for understanding true business performance. Cash flow analysis is enhanced by understanding the non-financial numbers behind the results. Forecasts of financial and non-financial indicators drive expectations of performance and thereby valuations.

Without this foundation, it would be impossible to truly discern good companies from bad ones, or worthy activities from poor ones. With a thorough understanding of performance measures and valuation, an entire framework for business planning can be built.

Why great stocks aren't often great companies – and vice versa

Can we rely on stock price as the ultimate indicator of company performance? For many reason, the answer is no. First, most companies don't have publicly traded stock to look at. There are literally millions of businesses in the USA that do not have a traded stock price. However, an understanding of what drives stock price valuations has lasting impact for business managers of private companies as well.

Even though, the largest and most well-known companies in the world do have stock prices to examine, a fundamental misunderstanding of stock *pricing* can persist.

What drives stock market valuations?

Managers express as much confusion about stock price as there appear to be misconceptions about strategy. CEOs of publicly-traded firms often lament the seeming disconnect between 'valuation and reality.'

> *'The market doesn't understand my company.'*

> *'We honestly have no idea what makes our company stock price go up or down. Sales are up. We thought showing large increases in net income would be good. But our stock price hasn't moved.'*

> *'My competitors have higher valuations. But everyone and their mother know that we are a better run, better-built company. So, I'd rather not have my employees focus on our stock price. It's distracting more than anything else.'*

In fact, these statements are far too kind. More management teams are heard to say a slightly more direct statement;

> *"The market is crazy."*

Who or what is a 'HOLT?'

The name HOLT is an acronym for the four founders of the firm that was launched in the 1980s that built the CFROI Framework and database. Bob Hendricks is the 'H' in 'HOLT.' To this day, Hendricks is a sought after advisor to some of the world's top-performing investment management firms. His stock-picking ideas and strategies are always held in high regard.

When meeting with stock analysts and investors who are young in their careers, Hendricks will provide this sage advice:

> *'One of the first things you have to become clear about is the difference between performance and valuation. Performance is historical and focuses on what the company has done. Valuation is about the future, about hope, about the company's prospects and forecasts.'*

Coca-Cola provides a great example that brings Hendrick's point home. In mid-1998, Coca-Cola's (KO's) stock price traded at an incredible high of $88 per share. About eight years later, Coca-Cola's stock price stood at about half of that mark, $44. Could Coca-Cola have lost its incredible competitive advantages? Did falling valuation imply poor performance?

The difference between a great company and a great stock

In spite of the valuation issues, Coca-Cola continues to generate CFROI results at some of the highest levels in the entire HOLT database of over 16,000 active companies. The flagship cola product is still heralded regularly as the world's top brand. Its venerable product distribution system may be called unparalleled. One of Coca-Cola's internal objectives has been to strive to ensure that 90% of the population of the USA is less than 50 feet away from a Coke product or a place to purchase one. So, what's the problem with KO?

Disciplined performance measurement and valuation implies a skill for deciphering the following problem: business profitability levels, and stock returns often seem to be greatly out of sync, and even totally disconnected.

Coca-Cola was a victim of its own great *prior* performance. At mid-year 1998, Coca-Cola was trading at a record high of $88 per share, having achieved record 40% cash flow returns. But at that share price, what did the market expect Coca-Cola to continue to do? In other words, what levels of performance would KO need to achieve to create the cash flows necessary to maintain its all-time stock price high?

KO's stock price at the time reflected cash flow return levels that would essentially never, ever fall. It also embedded significant organic growth of more than twice GDP levels for decades.

The problem was not that KO had not achieved incredible performance. The problem was a question as to whether that performance was sustainable. Even if sustainable, where was the upside in owning the stock with that level of expectation already built into the price? From a valuation perspective, there was really nowhere to go but down.

Eight years later we see the result of that unrealistic exuberance with a stock trading at half the price. This occurred – not because the company isn't a great one – but because the stock's valuation in 1998 was at the level of being fairly unjustifiable.

Great stock prices and great companies can accompany each other, but one needs to examine sufficiently long time periods. Over 20 years, KO is still outperforming the market by 2 or 3 times. That time period is marked with periods of unrealistic expectations, and so we see eight years of the stock falling.

Ames Department Stores

Around the same time as Coca-Cola's stock price hit its spectacular highs, a different, yet incredible stock price run was taking shape. A large regional discount retailer watched as its stock price soared from 1996 to 2000. Through that period, its shares rose more than tenfold, and investors and management seemed as happy as can be.

The retailer in question was not Wal-Mart, Costco, Best Buy, or any of the like. The firm was Ames Department Stores. Unfortunately, the epilogue is described too sadly by a string of empty buildings and emptier parking lots in strip malls across the Northeastern United States. By 2001, the firm had already been seeking bankruptcy protection. How could posted company performance and actual company stock price send such different messages?

At Ames, investor forecasts simply exceeded reality. The original march upward from lows of $2 in 1996 to $30 and higher was not because the company was incredibly profitable. During the five-year period, Ames's cash flow returns never once exceeded its cost of capital.

At $2, the stock was priced, for the most part, with the expectation that the firm would go into bankruptcy. However, Ames began avidly restructuring, divesting its least-performing assets. When a firm expected to go bankrupt *doesn't go bankrupt*, its stock price rises, sometimes by leaps and bounds.

At the time, an investor had to be confused, watching a retailer divest assets, close stores, yet demonstrate stock returns that were better than those of Wal-Mart. But stock prices are what they are for a reason. As expectations go from low to high, the stock price goes up. Or in this case, as expectations went from 'abysmal' to 'potential survival,' the stock price ran from $2 to over $40 per share.

The closure on this case is interesting because it shows the folly of management that does not understand the real drivers of stock price. Somehow, the company saw a signal to grow its business, and shifted its strategy to acquisitions and store openings in 1998 and 1999. The management team had previously shown discipline in shutting down problematic stores. By this time, it showed the folly of growing a business model that had not yet proven economically profitable. At no time did Ames's cash flow returns appear to exceed even lower bars of opportunity costs.

By 2000, that folly had run its course. Growing a bad business is always a bad thing, no matter how well the stock price is doing. Ames's death came relatively quickly, as the share price fell fast and the chain finally closed for good in late 2002.

The expectations conundrum

With valuation levels based on expectations of performance and not posted performance, there are troubling issues for investors and other decision-makers.

In 1998, when the stock market was booming into the tech bubble, a fundamentally based investor might have considered shorting a stock.

After all, many stocks seemed to have risen straight upward for several straight *years*. The market had priced in exuberant expectations.

However, if expectations had reached that high level, maybe they could still go to *ridiculously* exuberant levels before the bottom fell out, so to speak. The entire Internet bubble was a case study in this kind of market behavior.

How should a board member align management's interests with those of shareholders, when options and stock shares priced at such levels can only serve as reverse motivators? How can a company manager have the faith to know whether or not the right things are being done, when the stock begins to fall precipitously, despite profitability levels that remain the envy of the entire market?

Cash flows reveal the truth

Many examples exist of companies that are commonly thought to be great companies simply because they are great stocks, and vice versa. IBM and Federal Express stand out as two companies that continually receive high marks in the financial press such as 'most admired' status. However, a simple look at the firm's cash flows tells the tale: great turnarounds, not necessarily great companies. A series of other interesting examples are included at the back of this article.

Stock price alone can never reveal anything but changing expectations in a company's performance levels. By itself, stock price change says nothing about the level of performance.

Sharp investors live by something that many novice investors fail to understand: great companies can be terrible investments and vice versa. Therefore, great investments are made by better understanding the fundamentals behind the expectations. Those fundamentals need to be linked to long-term cash flow expectations, and only long-term forecasted cash flow analysis can explain the story that is built into any stock price.

The goal of corporate management remains the maximization of shareholder wealth, but that doesn't guarantee premium shareholder returns. The market's cash flow expectations set the bar that determines the company's future stock price returns, regardless of the caliber of the management team. In the end, knowing the difference between a great company and a great stock is what differentiates great managers and investors from poor ones.

Performance measures and Return Driven Strategy

One way to understand the importance of disciplined valuation and performance measurement is to relate performance measurement to the tenets and foundations of Return Driven Strategy. Note a clear linkage to some of the best practices in performance measurement and business execution.

Measures to Ethically Maximize Wealth

Businesses are driven in the direction they are steered. Performance measures provide the steering, guiding the organization into activities that are monitored in measurable results. However, what is the long-term direction in which a company must be guided?

The research behind the Return Driven Strategy framework tells us the highest tenet of business strategy: Ethically Maximize Wealth. Companies that abide by this rule show better financial results over long-term periods. Firms that do not live by this guiding principle comprise some of the worst financial performers ever. Given the importance of this tenet to success, what are the key performance measures that can guide and drive a firm's execution toward superior results?

Throughout this discussion, lagging and leading indicators are described in disciplined performance measurement. Lagging indicators help to understand what has happened in the past. Leading indicators provide insight to what may happen in the future. Attention to and balance of these types of performance measures are incredibly important for any organization.

First and foremost, companies must ensure that its business activities are aligned toward maximizing shareholder wealth. This must be done within the ethical parameters of the communities in which a company operates, or undue risk is accepted which can completely kill a company's valuation and ability to even stay in business. What performance measures can help ensure a company's attention to this all-important tenet of business strategy?

Discounted Cash Flows

If a firm is committed to maximize shareholder wealth, it must accept that valuation is a function of discounted cash flows, termed 'DCF.' To this end, every business must employ methods for tracking its ability to generate free cash flows over time in order to increase its DCF-based valuation. There are two important financial drivers that measure trend and level of cash flow performance.

Whether publicly or privately owned, investors need to know how much asset or investment growth is being made by management period-by-period. Second, the investor needs to under-stand how much cash the firm can generate over and above the investments it is making.

Depending on the industry and nature of the business, there are various ways of measuring investment and re-investment in a firm. Similarly, there are different ways of measuring the return on those investments. The nature of these calculations must be dependent not on some theoretical basis, but on an understanding of exactly how the metrics will be used to ensure that plans are executed.

Wealth Commitment

At times, certain measures are needed to ensure directional accuracy, such as for creating incentives in executive or employee compensation programs. Monitoring management compensation is key to understanding whether a firm will commit to maximize wealth. Whatever the measures, they must be theoretically and accurately consistent with the philosophy behind HOLT Relative Wealth Charts.

In order to Ethically Maximize Wealth, a firm must utilize the right incentives for executive, management, and employees. Are metrics unintentionally leading to unethical activities and behaviors that ultimately lead to disaster? Is management being paid to do things that are truly in the best, long-term interests of the shareholders? People do what they are paid to do. If their pay does not drive the first tenet of Return Driven Strategy, nothing else will.

Alignment

The widely used Balanced Scorecard framework is popular for directing management toward monitoring financial and non-financial measures of performance. The logic of the Balanced Scorecard is valid. Yet, management must ensure that strategic objectives and performance measures reflect the Commitment Tenet of Return Driven Strategy. If not, a manager must question the firm's ability to produce respectable returns for its shareholders. In well-designed Balanced Scorecards, certain measures explicitly target this tenet.

Beware of flawed financials

The highest tenet of Return Driven Strategy is to ethically manage for maximum wealth. This goal provides the anchor that will help management make the right decisions as they develop and execute business strategy. Strategic performance measures must be focused on maximizing financial value creation, something many companies fail to do because of misaligned compensation plans and/or misdirected motivations.

Performance measures can either lead to maximum wealth-creation, or they can create perverse incentives. Flawed financial metrics lead businesses in the wrong direction. Increases in revenues and earnings per share (EPS) are still widely reported as primary metrics of determining value creation, but when business decisions are based on those metrics, wealth-destroying activities have often resulted.

Value-destroying mergers and acquisitions can drive growth at the expense of cash flow returns. A strategy of under-investment, 'harvesting' assets, may increase accounting profits but actually destroy wealth for the long-term. In one study, Hewitt Associates found evidence that companies with management compensation highly aligned with traditional metrics, like sales and EPS, to be the worst performers in shareholder returns.

Performance measures and ethics

Companies must ensure adherence to the 'ethical component' of the first tenet of business strategy. A firm must develop and review performance measures or even 'markers' that indicate when activities are moving out of bounds of expected ethical behavior.

Companies that violate ethical behavior run the distinct risk of losing tremendous levels of value and even the ability to remain a going concern. Various performance measures can help track whether or not a firm is staying within the bounds of ethical behavior, as its communities define. This could include tracking litigation against the firm, monitoring trends in employee grievances, or watching for excessive or interest from consumer activist groups. Each of these may alert management to unhealthy trends.

Of course, one of the real concerns is the development of internal measures to monitor and control the financial reporting systems. When companies violate their trust with the investor markets through financial statement misreporting or fraud, they generate the close scrutiny and ire of the SEC and the shareholders, with drastic consequences.

Choosing the right direction

Managers who steer the firm wrong find them in a morass of poor financial performance with unhappy investors. Yet, the problem may not be in the ability to steer, but in choosing the wrong direction to drive in the first place. The Return Driven Strategy framework can accelerate the design and development of a performance measurement system.

Targeting superior financial results, the First Tenet of business strategy calls a company to 'Ethically Maximize Wealth.' Performance measures geared toward this goal can help drive an organization in the right direction. As drivers of the business, high-performance managers ask them if the right direction is set and if the performance measures really point there.

Tenets Two and Three

The pathway to superior financial performance is through the customer. Yet, what performance measures truly guide the organization to strategize and execute on this path? Companies naturally say they are focused on customers – but on which customers and what specific customer needs?

Research behind the Return Driven Strategy framework shows us that the most successful companies are guided by the goal tenets of business strategy: Fulfill Otherwise Unmet Customer Needs and Target Appropriate Customer Groups. History shows that these tenets must be the centerpiece for improving strategy and its execution. Given the importance, companies must understand how key performance measures can guide and drive a firm's execution toward superior results.

Customer needs, first and foremost

Most mediocre companies focus on performance measures relating to internal processes without a strong connection or linkage to customer need in the targeted market segments. Benchmarking and best practices are useful, but can lead a company in the wrong direction by focusing on the same processes and practices of the industry, unintentionally forgetting about the customer.

The high performance companies studied in the Return Driven Strategy Initiative do not make this mistake. The evidence shows, *"Focus first and foremost on customer need, and adjust internal processes appropriately."* This theme has helped many executive teams rethink the way they manage and measure performance, as well as rethink the way they interact and communicate with their customers.

GE's focus on one key strategic benchmark is now famous.

> *'Be number one or number two in the industry or get out.'*

This is a driving force for the business strategy of the organization. It is a customer-directed benchmark. Who but the customer makes the business unit number one? A company can innovate its processes or operate more efficiently, but none of this is of any worth if the customer isn't buying at prices close to the value received.

Customers vote in the form of purchases, choosing over any other competitor's offering. In its own way, this well-known statement drives the business toward a customer -focus.

Share of what?

When the management at the Coca-Cola learned that the average human being drinks 64 ounces of liquid per day, the goal became to increase Coke's 'share of stomach.'

But colas weren't enough to gain a higher percentage of those 64 ounces. So the company leveraged its marketing and distribution power to acquire and introduce new beverages: juices (Minute Maid, Fruitopia), coffee (Georgia, distributed in Japan), milk (Swerve), and water (Dasani), all in the name of capturing greater share of stomach worldwide.

Coca-Cola, amid concerns that it had saturated the soda pop beverage market, focused on this metric to help the company to continue growth beyond that core area. 'Share of stomach' or share of total beverages consumed, not simply soda pop, helped it to drive such businesses as its bottled water business and many other beverage lines. Unit sales and case sales have also been customer oriented, focusing on how consumers have voted for the company's products through their purchasing. Coca-Cola remains one of the most enviable examples of strategy and execution in all of Corporate America.

Communicating strategy

Many organizations do not effectively communicate strategy to employees. Often times, nebulous statements such as *"we seek profitable growth"* are used to explain strategy.

Employees do not implicitly understand the goals of the organization. While customers should naturally be considered the focus of attention, different business models based on different customer needs may require different activities – both strategically and in day-to-day operations. As strategies change, so must the measures employed to ensure change in an organization.

Performance measures that synchronize competencies

How well do existing performance measures enable the organization to synchronize the combination of competencies and supporting activities to fulfill unmet needs in large, growing customer groups?

High-performance firms align strategic activities with the right kinds of offerings. The most successful companies have been vigilant in detecting changing or unmet customer needs in large and high-growth customer groups.

Strategic performance measures should be closely focused around a line of sight, driven from the strategy. Michael Porter of Harvard Business School put it this way in an article entitled, 'The Importance of Being Strategic' in a 2002 Balanced Scorecard Report,

> *'Measure how various parts of your value chain actually fit together to lead to an overarching advantage, rather than using process-by-process metrics.'*

('The Importance of Being Strategic' Balanced Scorecard Report, March-April 2002).

No single measure is best in all situations

One performance metric cannot fit all situations. While there are a number of 'branded' performance measures with specific calculations, no single metric is ever best for every analysis, even within the boundaries of a single company or division. Performance metrics must be flexible to adapt to the purpose of the analysis required for resource allocation, executive compensation, business valuations, or other decisions.

Strategy first, then performance measures

Low-performing firms ignore this simple guideline. When installing or redesigning performance measures, the first questions some managers ask are the following:

"What should we measure?"

"How should we measure performance here?"

In fact, these are the last questions management should ask. Strategic performance measurement systems, like the Balanced Scorecard, are foremost about the implementation of strategy. Better questions to precede the establishment of performance measures might be the following:

"Have we explicitly defined our strategy and goals?"

"Do we understand the customer objectives, offering creation, and production objectives necessary to achieve our wealth-creation goals?"

Poorly-defined strategies lead to confusing and even contradictory performance measurement systems.

Metrics should change as strategy changes

Poor-performing organizations often use measures and benchmarks that are no longer relevant to their business strategy. Forces of change cause strategies to be outdated.

During the late 1990s, new technologies took center stage of most industries, reshaping the way companies conducted business and the demands consumers placed on the goods and services received.

Dell's initial strategy and performance measures differed from competitors like Compaq. Dell initially focused on operating effectively and efficiently. This involved shortening the cash conversion cycle by managing days' sales outstanding, days in inventory, and days' payables outstanding.

Later, when customers demanded more innovation of offerings in product and post-sales service, Dell needed to adjust its strategy and performance measures along with it.

Balanced Scorecard and Value-Based Management

The Balanced Scorecard and Value-Based Management (VBM) are two important innovations in performance measurement frameworks in the last twenty years. Many organizations have adopted one or both of these approaches in some way.

Both the Balanced Scorecard and VBM call for a hierarchy of measures and metrics, as one level of performance drive a secondary result. Employees that are trained well create more unique, customer-focused offerings. Singular need-fulfilling offerings lead to higher prices paid by customers. This leads to higher returns.

The performance measurement linkage and hierarchy at high-return organizations always followed the prioritization of importance implied by the stacked pyramid of tenets. Regardless of which branded system of performance measurement which a firm may use, the flow of performance must drive achievement of the tenets.

Concluding notes on Performance and Valuation

If it can't be measured, it can't be managed, and it certainly cannot be hoped to be valued. However, what exactly should be measured? The things that will most help the firm reach its higher goals, as outlined by the tenets of Return Driven Strategy. These lead to a more certain hope of achieving higher returns and wealth-creation, for the firm and its communities.

As the base foundation of the entire framework described in *Driven,* Disciplined Performance Measurement and Valuation is necessary to any great strategy. It is also necessary to the creation of any reliable or justifiable strategy framework.

In a world of so many business books and business frameworks, so many claim to profess the path to success. Many are consistent in nature. Many are conflicting in guiding the business leaders as to "what they should do."

In the end, any good leader will ask whether or not the process or activity will lead to higher performance in the future. That question lends itself to asking whether or not these have led to successful performance in the past.

If these measures of performance and valuation are not grounded in the reality of what actually drives the cash flows and values of firms over time, then any underlying model is suspect.

This final foundation is key to many issues in business strategy. It is paramount to the execution of the strategy, because what gets measured gets done, and if it cannot be measured it cannot be managed.

So, too, with a business strategy model. This foundation is the arbiter between what can trusted as a strategic analysis framework with a firm foundation, and one that cannot be relied on or only in limited circumstances.

If Return Driven Strategy is to be improved over the years to come, it is because of ongoing realization of the power of this foundation, and the actual performance results when applying the framework, as this Tenet, Disciplined Performance and Valuation, would have any reader come to expect.

Home Depot (HD)

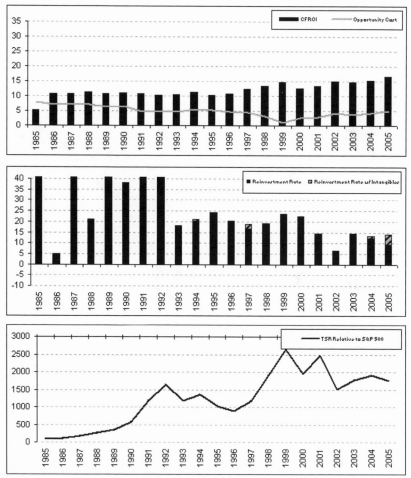

In search of a CEO in 2000, Home Depot found Bob Nardelli, a GE executive who brought with him Six Sigma expertise and other GE veterans. During his tenure, Home Depot built more new stores than had been built in the entire prior history. On top of that, the firm reached new CFROI heights on its entire store base, levels never previously achieved.

Critics cite the falling stock price from 2000 to 2007 as a representation of Nardelli's failings. On the contrary, Home Depot's stock price fell because the expectations that investors had built up in 2000 were probably unachievable by anyone. As CFROI levels and growth show, HD's performance was phenomenal with Nardelli, but not enough to live up to over-exuberant expectations set earlier. Changing forecasts drive stock prices, not necessarily immediate performance.

235

Emerson Electric (EMR)

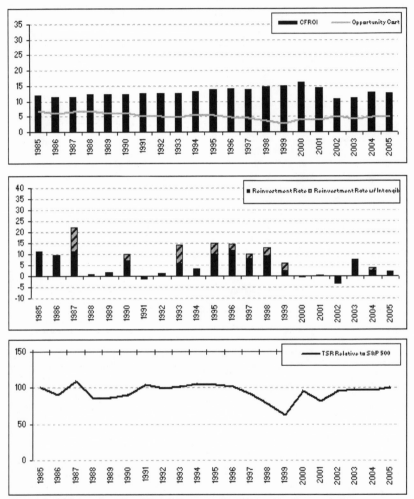

Emerson Electric is one of the icons of consistently high-performing industrials. With a twenty year CFROI pattern that has never fallen below 10%, and continual expansion through acquisitions and organic growth, the firm is a model of a well-run organization.

But, performance alone does not drive stock price, changing expectations do. 20 years ago, investors valued EMR with great expectations. As the company delivered on exactly those expectations, the stock price level was proven, and therefore remains stable with the market. As forecasts change, regardless of actual performance delivered, the stock price falls and rises, as 1996 to 2002 show.

United Technologies (UTX)

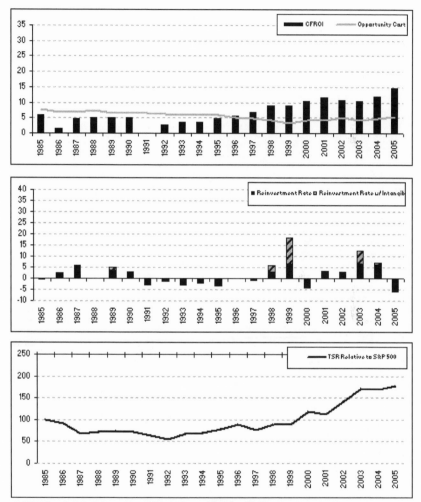

By 2005, after 20 years of turnaround work, United Technologies just reached the level of CFROI that Emerson Electric had been posting for two straight decades. Yet, because of UTX's poor performance in the 1980s, *investors had expected poor performance to continue,* pricing the stock low.

As UTX divested assets, shrinking to increase value when returns are low, the market began changing its forecasts for the future. When the firm began growing in 1998, with CFROI levels above the cost of capital, the market reset its forecasts upward again. The result was a rising stock price for 13 years. A company that goes from 'poor to better' can be a much better stock to own than an always great, yet stable, performer, such as EMR.

FedEx (FDX)

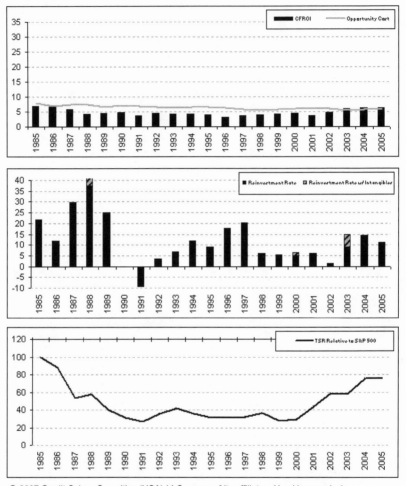

In recent history in the popular press and in business schools, probably no greater misunderstanding has arisen than the belief that FedEx's stock price from 2000 to 2006 was caused by great company performance. In fact, the firm's CFROI levels are average at best in 2004 and 2005, and well below corporate averages for the 20 years or more prior.

However, the FDX stock price was driven by a management team that took a poor 3% business to an average 6% level. That's the recipe for a great stock. Despite accolades for being the most admired, well-run business, the firm simply has never posted financial returns to justify that belief. Many other competitors in the industry have achieved higher returns for long periods of time.

Part Six

Conclusion

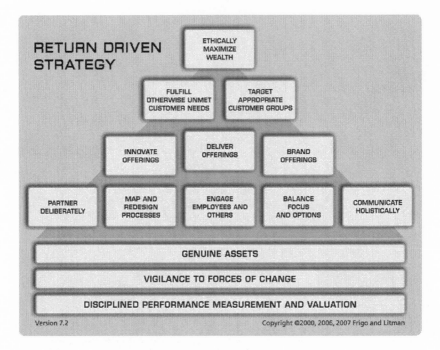

15

Conclusion
Applications of Return Driven Strategy

Today, Return Driven Strategy is being used in a number of applications. Clients, colleagues, and students of the framework have contributed greatly to its development through these varied uses.

In corporations

The framework is in use in strategic planning and management consulting at firms with revenues ranging from a few million dollars to billions annually. Some of these organizations have been large, publicly traded companies. Others have been privately-held or family-owned businesses.

Executives from a number of the world's largest and most successful companies – and from some of the most troubled – have attended Return Driven Strategy seminars, and spoken in panel discussions and speeches about the future of their firms.

To some degree, this book was written in response to the request of managers to have something to refer to after these seminars and workshops.

Strategic Risk Management

As directors and executives have used the framework to evaluate business strategy, they have also been able to hone in on key risks that could destroy shareholder value while considering the upside of risk in terms of the opportunities.

The alignment of enterprise risk management (ERM) with the Return Driven Strategy framework can enable managers to examine enterprise-wide risks more effectively. It can help to focus on risk management activities that ultimately protect or create value of the various constituents of the firm.

This can be a powerful method for evaluating the business. It has been used to proactively develop countermeasures for dealing with the risks that constantly threaten the achievement of enterprise objectives. The explicit linkage of risk and strategy should become an integral part of an organization's planning and review processes to help protect and create wealth.

In academia

Return Driven Strategy is being used in accredited graduate level business programs around the world, in various ways. In case studies, books, and presentations, content is being used in executive and MBA programs, in seminars and workshops, and at some of the world's top business schools. The model is central to the research conducted and published out of The Center for Strategy, Execution, and Valuation in Chicago.

Thousands of business students have taken courses, participated in seminars, and conducted research utilizing the framework, challenging it, and helping it to evolve. At DePaul University's Kellstadt Graduate School of Business, Return Driven Strategy is the centerpiece of an MBA concentration called 'SEV' for Strategy, Execution, and Valuation. It is the core focus of multiple graduate level MBA courses. A number of MBA students graduate annually with the SEV designation.

Career Driven Strategy

The application of the framework in career planning has been driven by the many MBAs who saw it as a natural fit for planning the right classes and designations for their jobs and careers.

Over the past few years, this has become a growing application of the model. Human Resources organizations and internal training programs have begun applying it in ways to help employees better understand their company strategies and how their roles can impact it. The framework appears to have value throughout the end-to-end employee life cycle from recruiting to hiring, training, developing, and engaging employees – and connecting with alumni.

In start-ups and new business initiatives

Return Driven Strategy has strong roots in the analysis of how venture capital firms succeed and what factors differentiate successful start-ups from failed ones. When used properly in the review of business plans, managers of start-up companies and new business initiatives have found the framework useful in for evaluating, planning, and modifying decisions at critical stages of the life cycle.

Many entrepreneurs have used Return Driven Strategy to evaluate new businesses prior to committing to investment. Seminars and workshops have been conducted as well as use by early start-up boards to better determine how and when to proceed. Literally thousands of business plans have been reviewed using the Return Driven Strategy model to identify key strengths and weaknesses of the plan.

In money management

The people at Credit Suisse, Credit Suisse HOLT, HOLT's clients, and other members of the HOLT community have contributed greatly to the content of Return Driven Strategy, particularly in the area of understanding the impact of corporate actions on stock price. The CFROI valuation model and database have been essential to the study of public company performance.

The marriage between strategy and valuation has made money management a natural arena for interest in the model. Money managers ranging from small hedge funds to giant institutional funds have attended conferences and seminars that include the content of Return Driven Strategy. Many investment firms have added elements of Return Driven Strategy into their investment thinking.

In nonprofit organizations, Mission Driven Strategy

Nonprofit organizations confront many of the same challenges as for-profit entities, as well some very unique ones. The Return Driven Strategy framework has been successfully adapted by a number of nonprofit organizations with the goal of maximizing mission-based value.

In executive workshops and board presentations at nonprofit organizations, the tenets, and foundations of Return Driven Strategy have helped management and board members to understand and refine strategy and make it more executable. So why do nonprofit organizations need Return Driven Strategy?

In some nonprofit organizations, strategic plans and activities are not focused on the true mission of the organization. Others have been focused on the wrong constituents. Still others have been overly attached to particular offerings or services that have become or are rapidly becoming obsolete.

For nonprofit organizations, the highest tenet of strategy is: 'Ethically Maximize Mission-Based Value.' This tenet provides the disciplined commitment to create value as defined by an organization's mission and to do so ethically. This means having the right goals, performance measures, alignment and structure to be able to achieve the goals.

An executive director of a large nonprofit posed the following question at a board meeting: *"Are we doing the right things for the right reasons?"* This is exactly the type of question Return Driven Strategy is designed to help answer. This nonprofit group has been using the framework for reviewing and designing their organizational plans.

What is the goal of the framework?

Business failure, in the long run, has dramatic negative impact on the business's communities. Resources are squandered, jobs are lost, and time is lost.

Business success, in the long run, is inseparable from the success of society. The title of the book *Driven* was chosen as *"Business Strat-*

egy, Human Actions, and the Creation of Wealth." Another title could easily have been, *"How to Succeed in a Free Market Economy."*

The more one studies the cash flows and valuations of a firm, the more obvious the role of human psychology and human behavior. By better understanding why people buy, why they work, and why investors invest, a business person can fulfill a key role in society by determining how to best fulfill the needs of these groups with the resources available.

Whether it sounds refreshingly insightful or cold and harsh, the flow of cash is not only a determining factor, but an unwavering measurement of whether or not a business and its managers are succeeding or failing in the roles they play for society. The free exchange of cash between various constituents signals the success or failure in the fulfillment of society's needs.

It is obvious that many areas of society do not naturally benefit from free markets. However, far more resources are available for those areas of society if the rest of society's resources are used most wisely. This occurs when customers, employees, and investors seek fulfillment of needs through freely chosen exchanges.

As authors, we hope that readers of *Driven* find benefits in the framework and this book's attempt at explaining it. As a guide for business planning, understanding human actions, and performance, we hope it can increase the ability of users of the framework to create wealth for them, as they do the rest of society, with all of us the better for it.

Frigo & Litman

Appendix:

A Primer for the Case Studies and Research in *DRIVEN*

How to understand a
HOLT Relative Wealth Chart

HOLT Relative Wealth Charts are used at the end of each tenet chapter and the end of the foundation of Disciplined Performance Measurement and Valuation.

The following primer describes how the charts show the economic performance of a firm. On the following pages, a panel-by-panel explanation describes how to read the three panels of a Relative Wealth Chart. These are the same charts that are in use by many of the world's largest and most influential investment firms when evaluating businesses and valuing stocks.

These charts display up to 21 years of performance in order to gauge economic cycles and provide better context for understanding the impact of short and long term business strategies.

(Relative Wealth Charts courtesy of Credit Suisse HOLT)

The top panel: CFROI® Levels

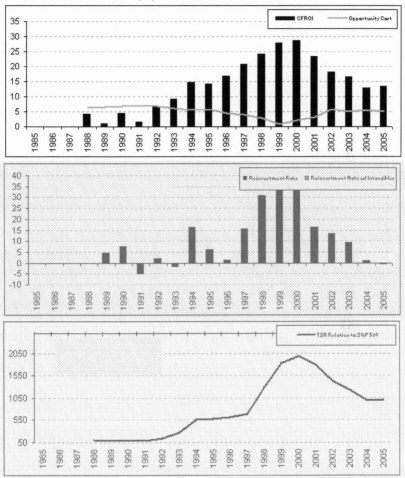

The top panel displays the CFROI® bars relative to the firm's opportunity cost of capital (opportunity cost line). The bars and the lines express percentages, adjusted for inflation. From 1993 to 2005, this example firm achieved a CFROI level well above the opportunity cost of the assets it used.

Looking at company performance is like looking at a personal savings account. The CFROI level is like the interest rate paid on a savings account. The opportunity cost line is similar in concept to the prevailing average rate. A good savings account pays above the average. A bad account pays below. The same can be said for a business, as a CFROI return should be above the opportunity cost of the assets that generated the returns.

The middle panel: Asset Growth/Reinvestment Rate

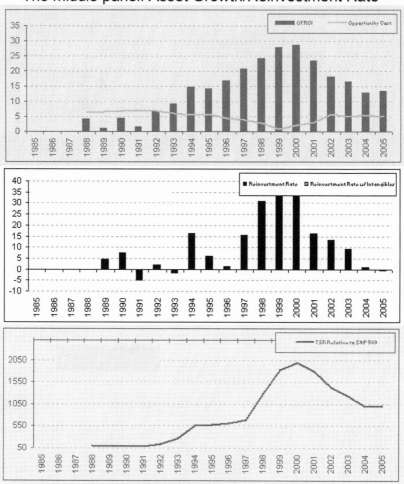

The middle panel displays 20+ years of a firm's asset growth rate, also known as the reinvestment rate. The bars tell how much the company is increasing or decreasing its asset base, expressed as a percentage compared to the prior year. Assets can be viewed just like the principal balance in a personal savings account. When the account pays more than the average, people should deposit more funds into the account and managers should find ways of deploying more assets at high return levels. When a savings account rate is below, people withdraw funds, as should managers withdraw assets.

In the above example, from 1989 to 1993, management correctly withheld investments. From 1997 to 2003, with such high returns, management compounded returns by reinvesting heavily. After 2000, management was unable to reinvest as quickly. However, given the falling CFROI levels, it might have been the only path available.

The bottom panel: Relative Total Shareholder Returns

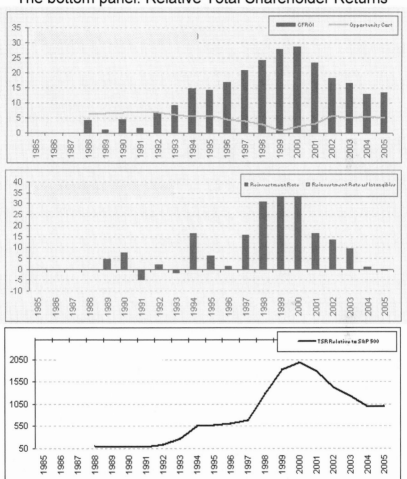

In the bottom panel, the line displays the upward and downward movement of the firm's stock price (and dividend payout) relative to the rest of the stock market's performance. The performance of the S&P 500 is used here as the benchmark for a firm to be compared. Stock price valuations change as investors *change their expectations of future performance*. This is driven in part by the top two panels that show historical performance.

In this example, investors' expectations, as seen in the stock price, move closely with the posted CFROI levels and growth rates. In the 1980s, dismal performance yielded low valuations. When the company posted peak returns and growth in 2000, investors expected the most, and stock price was highest. In 2005, lower returns and lower growth disappointed investors who priced the stock downward.

Summary of all three panels

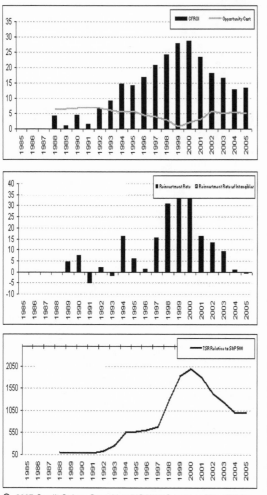

The top panel of the chart compares CFROI® level represented by the bars, to the Opportunity Cost of Capital, represented by the line, based on HOLT's calculations. An analogy would relate the CFROI measure to the interest paid by a savings account, while the cost of capital is related to an average bank interest rate. Rates higher than average are better. The comparison covers a history of the last 21 years.

The middle panel displays the reinvestment rate or growth in assets, represented by the bars. These should always be viewed in context of the CFROI levels in the top panel. In the savings account analogy, reinvestment rate is like an increase in prinicipal. If the interest rate is high, higher reinvestment rates create more value. If the interest rate is low, low or even negative investment is best.

The bottom panel displays annual changes in stock price valuation (including dividend payouts) relative to the return of a major stock market index, such as the S&P 500 in the USA. Stock price levels are driven by changing expectations of future CFROI returns and reinvestment rates. An upwardly sloping line is "beating the market." A downward sloping line is underperforming.

(This example features Nokia.)

A reason for the framework

Many people are "down" on the topic of business strategy: A few of the comments heard:

> *"When I hear the term 'business strategy,' I think of a bunch of high-priced consultants and fancy ideas that no one can implement."*

> *"...our strategic-planning process is 95% spreadsheet building, and only 5% really thinking about the future of the company."*

> *"I can tell you exactly what the company's strategy is right now. It's called 'Flavor of the Day.'"*

There is good reason for this cynicism. Often, so-called strategic initiatives do not pay off, despite countless hours and resources. At times, managers and employees are unable to reasonably understand how various strategic projects fit together.

In worst cases, new strategies have led to worse performance, negatively impacting business returns and employee compensation. People are left demoralized and unwilling to try anything new in the future.

A reason for managers' cynicism toward strategy is the set of misconceptions surrounding it. Many prevailing beliefs about 'good' businesses or strategies appear to be counter to the actual results they would hope to achieve.

Disciplined performance analysis is a necessary foundation for researching and building a superior strategic planning framework.

What is a return-driven business?

Return-driven businesses are those that plan and implement business activities consistently with the tenets and foundations and exhibit extraordinary financial results. These are the firms described in *Driven* as 'successful,' 'high-performance,' 'highly wealth-creating,' or similar terms. To be certain that these terms are being used accurately, there has been an unparalleled level of due diligence in the performance and value measurement of firms. 'Low-performing' or 'poor performance' labels have been given the same level of diligence. One can be assured that the company activities studied are being done so for the right reasons and in the right context.

'Returns' can refer to the monetary returns to investors for providing funds to the business. Returns also refer to the benefits customers receive for giving money in exchange for the business's offerings. The word 'return' also reflects the monetary and non-monetary compensation that employees and vendors receive when providing their time and efforts to the business.

When the constituents are receiving returns for these exchanges, we see sustained, high *cash flow returns on investment* within the business. The interaction of the cash flow returns and the resources invested in a business is invaluable in the determination of performance, both good and bad.

In high-performance return-driven businesses, one can see three main characteristics:

- Cash flow returns at levels well above the corporate averages (we often use a benchmark of "twice the average" to be certain). Cash flow returns need to be measured by tearing apart the financials line-by-line in order to distill economic reality from misleading accounting.

- Growth rates in the investments management is making in the business should exceed average market levels or other relevant growth benchmarks.

- Valuations that reflect investor's recognition of high return and growth sustainability – while not absolutely necessary to evaluate the success of a business, external business valuations can provide extraordinary insights into expected performance sustainability.

Firms Fade: High-performance is not permanent

In the case studies at the end of each chapter, a specific period of performance is cited with the relevant plans and activities that led to that performance period, good or bad.

Over a long enough period of time, it would appear that even the companies with the greatest performance for a set period of time do not sustain it indefinitely. In some cases, the growth engine continues, but returns fade. In others, returns sustain, but growth shuts off.

When firms fade in performance, the pathway can be charted to examples of how the tenets in the Return Driven Strategy framework have been neglected, or have simply become unachievable for that business. Meanwhile, the rise of companies and the sustainability of high-performance can be attributed to attention and execution of the framework.

Examples of companies at wide ranges of the performance spectrum are discussed in *Driven*. Many more are included in articles and available through www.returndriven.com and other online sources.

Research and ongoing application

The insights of a business planning framework can only be as good as the link they have to actual cash flow performance. If the underlying financial acumen is strong, the analysis can better be relied on. If weak, then one can have little assurance that a particular action will result in the desired outcome.

If Return Driven Strategy offers something different to business managers and analysts, it's a level of confidence that the activities guided by this framework will have a better likelihood of achieving the desired, wealth-creating results.

Return Driven Strategy evolves from a consortium of professional and academic sources. It has been tested and refined in private and public company applications by management teams of publicly-traded and privately-held firms in a wide spectrum of industries and locations.

Management consultants have worked with the framework and also provided additional perspectives.

The framework contains insights from working with investors and investment advisors, including stock analysts and money managers in firms of all sizes, including some of the most influential funds in the world. This included studies from and discussions with private equity firms and venture capitalists.

Return Driven Strategy benefited greatly from the studies, insights, databases, people, and client network of Credit Suisse HOLT. The CFROI® model and global company database continue to provide extensive cash flow analysis of thousands of firms. The CFROI® Framework is one of the most advanced, comprehensive, and reliable ever built. In *Driven,* case studies of *Relative Wealth Charts* provide a small glimpse into the power of this cash flow framework.

The framework's tenets and foundations have been tested and refined in extensive use in the vetting and testing of new business plans and launches – and in evaluating start-up firms, very early in their life cycle. The evolution of this framework reflects insights from the examination of the business plans of thousands of new companies.

In start-ups and large-public companies alike, the tenets and foundations of Return Driven Strategy were found to be consistent in every successful business, regardless of size, scope, industry, or geography. Firms that create wealth follow the same basic rules of wealth-creation, regardless of these differences.

Book Endnotes

Different analysis yields different conclusions. During the last three decades, there have been many attempts to study high performance companies.

An article in *Harvard Business Review* (Kirby, Julia, "Toward a Theory of High Performance" *Harvard Business Review,* 2005) profiled some of these studies, including: Peters, Thomas J. and Robert H. Waterman, *In Search of Excellence: Lessons from America's Best-Run Companies,* Harper & Row, 1982; Kotter, John P. and James L. Heskett, *Corporate Culture and Performance,* Free Press, 1992; Collins, James C. and Jerry I. Porras, *Built to Last: Successful Habits of Visionary Companies,* HarperBusiness, 1994; Jain, Arun Kumar, *Corporate Excellence,* Excel Books, 1998; Katzenbach, Jon R. *Peak Performance: Aligning the Hearts and Minds of Your Employees,* Harvard Business School Press, 2000; Foster, Richard and Sarah Kaplan, *Destruction: Why Companies That Are Built to Last Underperform the Market-and How to Successfully Transform Them,* Currency, 2001; Zook, Chris and James Allen, *Profit from the Core: Growth Strategies in an Era of Turbulence,* Harvard Business School Press, 2001; Joyce, William, Nitin Nohria and Bruce Roberson, *What Really Works: The 4+2 Formula for Sustained Business Success,* HarperBusiness, 2003; Breene, R. Timothy and Paul F. Nunes, Accenture Published Materials. More recent works include: Kim, W. Chan and Renee Mauborgne, *Blue Ocean Strategy: How to Create Uncontested Market Space and Make the Competition Irrelevant,* Harvard Business School Press, 2005 and Collins, James C. *Good to Great: Why Some Companies Make the Leap and Others Don't,* HarperBusiness, 2001.

Each of these works has made certain contributions. Yet the question and comment by Julia Kirby in *Harvard Business Review* guides future work and inquiry: "What does it mean to be a high-performance company? Twenty-three years after In Search of Excellence, we're still searching—and just maybe getting closer to answers." One of the intentions of this book is to describe what it means to be a high-performance company in terms of performance metrics and the strategic activities and traits that led to sustained periods of exceptionally high performance in terms of return on investment, growth, and wealth creation.

For a discussion of the connection between strategy and valuation see Litman, Joel and Mark L. Frigo "When Strategy and Valuation Meet: Five Lessons from Return Driven Strategy" *Strategic Finance,* 2004.

For a discussion of the calculation and philosophy of the CFROI measure, see Madden, Bartley J. *CFROI Valuation: A Total System Approach to Valuing the Firm.* Woburn: Butterworth-Heinemann, 1999; Madden, Bartley J. *Maximizing Shareholder Value And The Greater Good.* Naperville: LearningWhatWorks, 2005

For more on the ideas behind freedom and wealth creation, see Friedman, Milton *Capitalism and Freedom.* Chicago: The University of Chicago Press, 1962; Friedman, Milton and Rose Friedman *Free To Choose: A Personal Statement.* New York: Harvest, Harcourt Inc., 1990.

For a discussion of private versus public ownership issues, see Frigo, Mark L and Joel Litman "Give My Regrets to Wall Street" *Harvard Business Review,* 2004.

For a discussion of Warren Buffett's philosophy, see Lowe, Janet *Warren Buffett Speaks-Wit and Wisdom from the World's Greatest Investor.* New York: John Wiley & Sons, Inc., 1997

For a discussion of the great product conundrum see Litman, Joel and Mark L. Frigo. "When Strategy and Valuation Meet: Five Lessons from Return Driven Strategy" *Strategic Finance,* 2004.

For more information on voice-based communication analysis technologies, see Fickes, Michael "What is truth?" *Government Security,* 2004; Joe, Ryan "Listening for Lies" *Speech Technology,* 2007.

Targeting appropriate customer groups and being the dominant provider of offering to targeted customer groups is critical for every organization. The focus on "Be number 1 or number 2 or get out" at General Electric was something Jack Welch credited to Peter Drucker, the father of modern management. Peter Drucker's question for management was: "If you weren't already in the business, would you enter it today?" (see Drucker, Peter F. *Innovation and Entrepreneurship: Practice and Principles*. London: William Heinemann. 1985; Drucker, Peter F. *Managing for the Future: The 1990s and Beyond.* New York: Truman Talley Books, Dutton, 1992; Welch, Jack. *Jack: Straight from the Gut* New York: Warner 2001).

Bibliography

Ansoff, H. Igor. *Corporate Strategy: An Analytic Approach to Business Policy for Growth and Expansion.* New York: McGraw Hill. 1965

Beasley, Mark S. and Mark L. Frigo, "Strategic Risk Management: Creating and Protecting Value" *Strategic Finance,* 2007

Bell, C. Gordon and John E. McNamara. *High-Tech Ventures: The Guide for Entrepreneurial Success.* Reading: Perseus Books, 1991

Bossidy, Larry and Ram Charan, *Execution: The Discipline of Getting Things Done.* New York: Crown Business, 2002

Bruce, Brian R. and Mark T. Bradshaw *Analysts, Lies and Statistics.* New York: Institutional Investor Books, 2004

Cialdini, Robert B. *Influence: Science and Practice.* Needham Heights: Allyn and Bacon, 2001

Christensen, Clayton M. and Michael E. Raynor. *The Innovator's Solution: Creating and Sustaining Successful Growth.* Boston: Harvard Business School Press, 2003

Davenport, Thomas H. and Jeanne G. Harris, *Competing on Analytics: The New Science of Winning.* Boston: Harvard Business School Press, 2007

Downes, Larry and Chunka Mui. *Unleashing the Killer App.* Boston: Harvard Business School Press, 1998

Drucker, Peter F. *Innovation and Entrepreneurship: Practice and Principles.* London: William Heinemann. 1985

Drucker, Peter F. *Managing for the Future: The 1990s and Beyond.* New York: Truman Talley Books, Dutton, 1992

Drucker, Peter F. *Innovation and Entrepreneurship: Practice and Principles*. London: William Heinemann, 1985

Epstein, Barry J., Ralph Nach and Steven M. Bragg. *Wiley GAAP 2006*.Hoboken: John Wiley and Sons, Inc., 2005

Epstein, Marc J. *Making Sustainability Work: Best Practices in Managing and Measuring Corporate, Social, Environmental and Economic Impacts.* Sheffield, UK: Greenleaf Publishing, 2008

Foster, Richard and Sarah Kaplan. Creative Destruction. New York: Doubleday, 2001

Friedman, Milton *Capitalism and Freedom.* Chicago: The University of Chicago Press, 1962

Friedman, Milton and Rose Friedman *Free To Choose.* New York: Harvest, Harcourt Inc., 1990

Frigo, Mark L and Joel Litman "Give My Regrets to Wall Street" *Harvard Business Review,* 2004

Frigo, Mark L. "What is Mission Driven Strategy?" *Strategic Finance,* 2003

Gladwell, Malcolm. *The Tipping Point: How Little Things Can Make a Big Difference.* New York: Little Brown & Company, 2000

Goldratt, Eliyahu M. *Theory of Constraints.* Great Barrington: North River Press, 1990

Goldratt, Eliyahu M. and Jeff Cox *The Goal. A Process of Ongoing Improvement.* Great Barrington: The North River Press, 1992

Goleman, Daniel. *Emotional Intelligence.* New York: Bantam Books, 1997

Goleman, Daniel. *Working with Emotional Intelligence.* New York: Bantam Books, 2000

Humes, James C. *Speak Like Churchill, Stand Like Lincoln*. Roseville: Prima Publishing, 2002

Kaplan, Robert S., and David P. Norton. *Alignment: Using the Balanced Scorecard to Create Corporate Synergies*. Boston: Harvard Business School Press, 2006

Kaplan, Robert S., and David P. Norton. "The Balanced Scorecard – Measures that Drive Performance." *Harvard Business Review*, 1992

Kirby, Julia, "Toward a Theory of High Performance" *Harvard Business Review*, 2005

Kotter, John P. and James L. Heskett. *Corporate Culture and Performance*. New York: Free Press, 1992

Levitt, Theodore. "Marketing Myopia." *Harvard Business Review*, 1975

Litman, Joel and Mark L. Frigo "When Strategy and Valuation Meet: Five Lessons from Return Driven Strategy" *Strategic Finance*, 2004

Lowe, Janet. *Warren Buffett Speaks – Wit and Wisdom from the World's Greatest Investor*. New York: John Wiley & Sons, Inc., 1997

Madden, Bartley J. *CFROI Valuation A Total System Approach to Valuing the Firm*. Woburn: Butterworth-Heinemann, 1999

Madden, Bartley J. *Maximizing Shareholder Value And The Greater Good*. Naperville: LearningWhatWorks, 2005

Mitchell, Jack, *Hug Your Customers: The Proven Way to Personalize Sales and Achieve Astounding Results*, New York: Hyperion, 2003

Peters, Thomas J. and Robert H. Waterman. *In Search of Excellence: Lessons from America's Best-Run Companies*. New York: Harper & Row, 1982

Porter, Michael E. "The Importance of Being Strategic" *Balanced Scorecard Report*, Harvard Business School Press, 2002

Porter, Michael E. "What is Strategy?" *Harvard Business Review*, 1996

Porter, Michael E. *Competitive Advantage-Creating and Sustaining Superior Performance*. New York: The Free Press, 1985

Porter, Michael E. *Competitive Strategy Techniques for Analyzing Industries and Competitors*. New York: The Free Press, 1980

Reichheld, Fred. *The Ultimate Question Driving Good Profits and True Growth*. Boston: Harvard Business School Press, 2006

Reid, Peter C. *Well Made in America: Lessons from Harley-Davidson on Being the Best*. New York: McGraw-Hill Publishing, 1990

Ries, Al and Laura Ries. *The 22 Immutable Laws of Branding.* New York: HarperCollins Publishers Inc., 1998

Salovey, Peter, Marc A. Brackett and John D. Mayer. *Emotional Intelligence: Key Readings on the Mayer and Salovey Model* Port Chester: Dude Publishing, 2004

Schumpeter, Joseph A. *The Theory of Economic Development.* Cambridge: Harvard University Press, 1934

Schumpeter, Joseph A. *Capitalism, Socialism and Democracy.* New York: HarperCollins Publishers Inc., 1975 (originally published 1942)

Surowiecki, James. *The Wisdom of Crowds.* New York: Doubleday, 2004

Slywotzky, Adrian J. *The Upside: The 7 Strategies for Turning Big Threats Into Growth Breakthroughs*. New York: Crown Business, 2007

Ulrich, Dave and Norm Smallwood, *Leadership Brand: Developing Customer-Focused Leaders to Drive Performance and Build Lasting Value*. Boston: Harvard Business School Press, 2007

Walton, Mary. *The Deming Management Method.* New York: Perigee Books, 1986

Welch, Jack. *Jack: Straight from the Gut.* New York: Warner 2001

Zook, Chris and James Allen, *Profit from the Core: Growth Strategies in an Era of Turbulence.* Boston: Harvard Business School Press, 2001

Zyman, Sergio. *The End of Advertising As We Know It.* Hoboken: John Wiley and Sons, Inc., 2002

INDEX

About the Authors

Mark L. Frigo is Director of The Center for Strategy, Execution, and Valuation in the Kellstadt Graduate School of Business at DePaul University and Ledger & Quill Alumni Foundation Distinguished Professor of Strategy and Leadership. Author of six books and over 70 articles, his work is published in leading journals including *Harvard Business Review*. Dr. Frigo is a frequent contributor and an editor for *Strategic Finance* and lectures at universities and conferences throughout North America and Europe. He is a leading expert on strategy and execution in high-performance companies and strategic risk management.

His professional career has included corporate strategic planning, mergers and acquisitions, and management consulting in strategic services at an international consulting firm. Dr. Frigo is recipient of the Economos Award for outstanding teaching in the Kellstadt Graduate School of Business MBA program, awards by professional organizations for his executive education programs and he was recently profiled in *Crain's Chicago Business* in an article about top Business School professors.

He received his Bachelor of Science degree in Accountancy from the University of Illinois, an MBA degree from Northern Illinois University and completed postgraduate studies in the Kellogg Graduate School of Management at Northwestern University. He is a CPA in the State of Illinois and a Certified Management Accountant. Dr. Frigo received his Ph.D. in Econometrics. He serves as an advisor to senior executive teams and boards of directors.

Joel Litman is a Director at HOLT, a corporate performance and valuation advisory service of Credit Suisse, a global financial services company. Joel advises investment managers including pension funds and hedge funds in their investment processes and business management. Prior to Credit Suisse, Joel spent ten years providing corporate financial advisory services and consulting management teams of large corporations, privately-held businesses, and venture capital-backed firms.

Joel is a leading practitioner of the CFROI® Valuation framework as well as other performance and valuation methodologies. He is a founder of The Center for Strategy, Execution, and Valuation in Chicago.

He has been editor or author of articles in publications including *Harvard Business Review, Strategic Finance Magazine, Insight*, and others. His articles include 'When Strategy and Valuation Meet,' 'Why Great Stocks Aren't Always Great Companies,' and 'Give My Regrets to Wall Street.'

Joel is Clinical Professor of Business Strategy at DePaul's Kellstadt Program, where he helped to create a new MBA concentration and was named Adjunct Professor of the Year. He has spoken at universities including Harvard, University of Chicago, Wharton, MIT Sloan, London Business School, and UIBE in Beijing, China and at corporate and trade association events around the world.

Joel is a CPA in the State of Illinois, received his B.S in Accounting from DePaul University and MBA from the Kellogg Graduate School of Management at Northwestern University.

11820131R0018

Made in the USA
Lexington, KY
04 November 2011